CHAPTER 1

LOOKING AT YOUR ORCHIDS

There is a multitude of fine wines available, and many are more expensive than the champagne you will find on the shelves at your local supermarket. But the word 'champagne' has a special magic. And so it is with the word 'orchid' — the champagne equivalent in the world of plants.

Before World War II orchids were plants for dedicated hobbyists, sold by specialist nurseries to people who could afford the high prices — the first edition of The House Plant Expert did not include them. Things are now so different — they have become one of the top three favourite pot plants and they are sold in supermarkets, hardware outlets, florists and garden centres everywhere. What happened?

It is all down to a small group of orchids which are mass produced and are on display wherever house plants are sold. They are well suited to growing under living room conditions and they are no more expensive than many other indoor plants. This orchid revolution has been led by *Phalaenopsis* — the Moth Orchid, and followed by the Slipper Orchid (*Paphiopedilum*).

You can treat these two plants as long-lasting but still temporary residents of your living room. They will stay in bloom for one or even several months, but are then thrown away like the Pot Chrysanthemums, Azaleas and Poinsettias. You can go a step further, however — with a few simple techniques you can get them to bloom again, and so transform them into permanent members of your household. And you can add other orchids which you should be able to buy locally, such as *Cymbidium*, Cambria and *Oncidium*. A disappointing fact here is that you will not be told the species or hybrid name. Part of the fun of growing roses, bulbs, trees etc is to know the variety or hybrid you are growing, but with your shop-bought orchid the label will say 'Moth Orchid', 'Phalaenopsis' or just 'Orchid'.

A much wider range of types can be grown if you have a greenhouse — the ones to choose will depend on the winter temperature you can maintain. You will find details in this book, together with information on how to find suppliers of the many beautiful orchids which are now available.

And so you, like countless others before you, may move from the possession of a single Moth Orchid to be the owner of a varied orchid collection which is in bloom nearly all year round. Some will be easier to grow than almost any other pot plant and others will offer a challenge which will test your green fingers to the limit, but all will be fascinating.

Fascinating because orchids really are different. No other plants have their flower anatomy or their complex seed germination story. Among the various types you will find roots which can take in moisture from the air, flowers which last for months and colour combinations which are unmatched in the plant kingdom.

So orchids are special, but the commercially-cultivated ones represent only a tiny fraction of the orchid story. There are plants which can fit in an egg cup to those which weigh more than a ton, and flower sizes from a pin head to a dinner plate. There are about 800 different natural genera and hundreds of genera created by hybridists. There are nearly 30,000 species and more than 100,000 named hybrids. And the list continues to grow as new species are discovered and new hybrids are introduced. They are found from the arctic to the equator, but nearly all are too small or too plain to be raised for sale — these are the botanicals.

The decision whether to grow orchids or not is up to you, but it should not be influenced by the old idea that they are too difficult for ordinary people. The popular ones are no more difficult than the average house plant. The next stage for many is building up a collection, and this can be an engrossing hobby — the final stage is propagating your own plants, and here is the real challenge. The orchid, as ever, remains a plant of mystery.

UNDERSTANDING ORCHID NAMES

The naming of orchids is more complex than the way we describe other garden and indoor plants. The reason is that there is a multitude of natural species and varieties, together with an abundance of hybrids of different species, different hybrids and even different genera. In addition different forms of these hybrids have often been named and offered for sale. Complex, but the basic principles are not difficult to understand.

SPECIES ORCHIDS   'Natural' types which grow or have grown in the wild

Example:

Dendrobium	*wardianum*	var. *album*
GENUS: Written in italics with a capital letter	**SPECIES:** Written in italics without a capital letter	**VARIETY:** Written in italics without a capital letter
The genus is like a family name — many members may share the same name. *Dendrobium* has more than 1000 species.	The species is like a given name — these are types of the genus which have one or more features which are different.	The variety is a form of the species which is not different enough to be classed as a separate species.

HYBRID ORCHIDS

'Created' types which have resulted from the crossing by the breeder of two or more different cultivars, grex, varieties, species or genera

Example:

Vuylstekeara	Cambria	'Plush'
GENUS: Written in italics with a capital letter. x is sometimes used to denote a hybrid genus	**HYBRID GROUP** or **GREX:** Written in roman (upright) type with a capital letter	**CULTIVAR:** Written in roman (upright) type with a capital letter and inverted commas
The genus may be 'natural', or it may have been created by crossing two or more genera. The name of a bigeneric hybrid combines the names of the two parent genera — e.g *Laeliocattleya*. A trigeneric hybrid combines all three generic names — e.g *Brassolaeliocattleya*. This system would be too unwieldy where there are four or more parent genera. Here the name of a person is used, plus –ara at the end — e.g *Vuylstekeara*.	The hybrid group is a cross between species and/or hybrids. A primary hybrid is a cross between two species. At first hybrid groups were given latin-sounding names, but this is no longer allowed.	A cultivar is a form which has been selected from the hybrid group because it has one or more desirable properties.

Moreton Morrell Site

The ORCHID EXPERT

Dr

First Edition: 50,000 copies

Published by Expert Books
a division of Transworld Publishers

TRANSWORLD PUBLISHERS
61-63 Uxbridge Road, London W5 5SA
a division of the Random House Group Ltd

Distributed in the United States
by Sterling Publishing Co. Inc.
387 Park Avenue South,
New York,
NY 10016-8810

Contents

Reproduction by Spot On Digital Imaging Ltd, Gomm Road, High Wycombe, Bucks HP13 7DJ
Printed and bound by Mohn Media Mohndruck GmbH

ISBN 978 0 903505 67 3

NATURAL HABITATS

Nearly all of the orchids you will see are epiphytes, but a few important ones such as *Paphiopedilum* and *Phragmipedium* are ground dwellers.

EPIPHYTIC ORCHIDS
These plants grow on trees and may reach a great size. All are tropical or subtropical and are not parasitic. Roots grip the bark, and there are also fleshy aerial roots which take in moisture as well as nutrients derived from rotting plant litter and bird droppings.

LITHOPHYTIC ORCHIDS
These plants grow on bare rock or the mossy covering.

TERRESTRIAL ORCHIDS
These plants grow at ground level, usually in the surface layer of plant litter. All temperate orchids are terrestrial — the leaves die down in winter.

GROWTH TYPES

Most of the orchids you can buy have a sympodial growth habit. However, there are a few important genera such as *Phalaenopsis* and *Vanda* which have a monopodial growth habit.

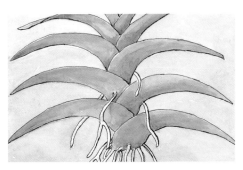

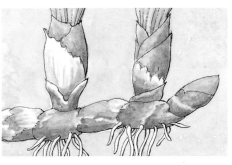

MONOPODIAL GROWTH
The plant grows upright, not sideways. The single stem continues to grow year after year from the apex — leaves are carried on either side and aerial roots are borne along the lower part. Flowers appear from between the leaves. They do not all look alike when not in flower — some grow tall with a regular leaf pattern (e.g *Vanda*) while others such as *Phalaenopsis* are compact with little upright growth and only a few leaves.

SYMPODIAL GROWTH
The plant grows sideways, not upright. Pseudobulbs (see page 7) are connected by thick horizontal stems known as rhizomes. New growth takes place from a bud at the base of a leading pseudobulb and this new rhizome develops a pseudobulb at its tip. This may be right next to the mother pseudobulb or some distance away from it. From this pseudobulb the leaves and flower spike appear.

PLANT ANATOMY

There is no single universal feature to tell you that the flowerless plant you are looking at is an orchid. All the veins may run straight down the leaf, but this property is shared with all the monocotyledons like tulips and irises. There is very likely to be pseudobulbs present, but this is not a certain guide as there are some popular orchids where this feature is missing.

It is the flower which is unique, as only orchids possess a column (see page 8). The sole purpose of the flower in nature is to ensure a visit by the required pollinator which will transfer pollen from another orchid to the stigma of the female reproductive organ. The pollinator is usually just one type of butterfly, moth etc. These insects may not be numerous and the plant may not be easy to reach, and so some orchids have evolved with large, colourful and long-lasting flowers.

The various ways orchids have devised to attract and in some cases to hold insects in order to ensure pollination are always interesting and sometimes amazing — see page 9.

Nearly all the popular orchids are sympodial types with pseudobulbs. This classic type is illustrated below.

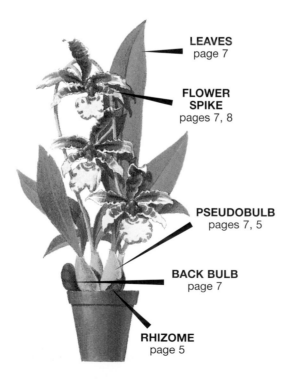

LEAVES
page 7

FLOWER SPIKE
pages 7, 8

PSEUDOBULB
pages 7, 5

BACK BULB
page 7

RHIZOME
page 5

ROOTS

The roots of tree-dwelling orchids are thick and hairless, which mean that they require their own special growing medium. The root is covered with velamen — a soft layer which can absorb and retain moisture. When wet this layer becomes partly transparent to reveal the green tissue below — the tip of the root is green when actively growing. These roots arise from the pseudobulbs and are active for only one season.

The roots of ground-dwelling orchids are different — they are either numerous and thin arising from underground tubers, or thicker and fleshy growing from the base of the plant.

LEAVES

The leaves arise from the top of the pseudobulb. Their role on the plant is nearly always functional with no decorative value, but a few orchids such as *Ludisia* are grown primarily for the beauty of their foliage. There is a larger group which are grown for both leaves and flowers — the mottle-leaved *Paphiopedilum* hybrids are an example.

There is a wide variety of shapes, sizes and colours. Examples of the many types are plicate (pleated), terete (pencil-like), soft-textured (fleshy) and hard-textured (leathery). A change in colour is one of the indicators of poor growing conditions.

TUBER

Terrestrial orchids growing in temperate regions have round underground tubers instead of pseudobulbs to serve as water- and nutrient-holding reservoirs. Leaves fall in winter and the orchid remains dormant in this state. In spring the tuber produces new stems and roots.

BACK BULB

A leafless and non-functioning pseudobulb. The back bulbs of some orchids can be used for propagation — see page 37.

FLOWER SPIKE

The spike consists of the flower stem and the buds and blooms it bears. It is a non-technical term which is universally used by orchid growers — to the botanist it means something different (see below). Some beautiful orchids produce a single bloom on top of the stem — others bear several or many in an inflorescence (flower head). The usual arrangement is a raceme.

SPIKE	**RACEME**	**PANICLE**	**CYME**
Stalkless or almost stalkless flowers borne on the stem	Like a spike, but flowers are borne on short stalks	Like a raceme, but each stalk bears a miniature raceme	A flower head usually domed or flattened — stalks arise from different points

PSEUDOBULB

This swollen flower base is found on nearly all tropical and sub-tropical orchids which live on trees. Roots grow from the base, between one and a dozen leaves appear from the top and the flower stem grows from the base, top or sides. Its purpose is to store water in order to allow the plant to survive during periods of dry weather. A bud at the base of the current pseudobulb will produce next year's rhizome and pseudobulb. After several years the pseudobulb dies and remains attached to the plant as a back bulb. Pseudobulbs come in various shapes and sizes, as illustrated below:

ROUND or OVAL	**FLATTENED**	**CANE-LIKE**	**RIBBED**	**CLUB-SHAPED**	**ABSENT**
Example: *Encyclia*	Example: *Miltonia*	Example: *Dendrobium*	Example: *Stanhopea*	Example: *Cattleya*	Example: *Paphiopedilum*

FLOWER ANATOMY

However tiny or large, however simple or ornate, all orchids have the same basic pattern. Each side is a mirror image of the other, and the parts are in threes.

In bud the flower is protected by an outer ring of three sepals and within is a ring of three petals. These plant parts show a bewildering range of variations. The lip is usually showy but in a few genera (e.g *Vanda* and *Ascocenda*) it is small. The sepals are usually free, but two (e.g *Paphiopedilum*) or all three (e.g *Masdevallia*) may be fused. In the centre of the flowers is a unique feature — the column.

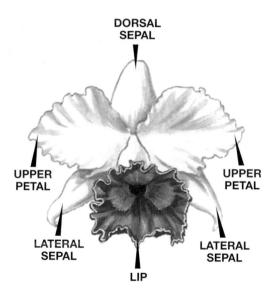

DORSAL SEPAL

UPPER PETAL

UPPER PETAL

LATERAL SEPAL

LATERAL SEPAL

LIP

LIP
This third petal (called the lip or labellum) is quite unlike the two upper petals. It generally serves as a landing platform for a fly, butterfly or moth — there may be colourful honey guides to direct the pollinator to the sexual organs on the column. Some lips are able to move in the breeze and so add to the insect mimicry of the flowers (see page 9). One of the most dramatic forms is the pouched lip found in the Slipper Orchids.

COLUMN
A rod-like structure at the centre of the flower — it is a fusion of both the male and female reproductive organs. At the top of the column is the anther which produces pollen — the fine grains are bound together as small balls known as pollinia. Below is the stigma — a sticky plate to which the pollinium carried by the pollinating insect is transferred.

SEED
After pollination the flower dies and the capsule (commonly referred to as a pod) develops. Within this fruit the seeds form — up to 4 million and as fine as dust. They hold no food supplies and will not germinate in ordinary soil or compost — see page 43.

SPUR
Many orchids bear a tubular extension at the back of the lip or some other flower part. It carries nectar and so acts as an attractant to pollinating insects. The spur is often small and insignificant, but it grows to 1 ft (30 cm) or more in some species of *Angraecum*.

FLOWER SIZE

UPSIDE-DOWN FLOWERS
With nearly all orchids the lip is uppermost at the bud stage. As the flower opens the stalk attaching it to the stem turns through 180° so that the lip in the open flower is at the base of the bloom. This process is known as **resupination**.

SMALL
under 2 in. (5 cm)

MEDIUM
2-3 in. (5-7.5 cm)

LARGE
over 3 in. (7.5 cm)

POLLINATION

All the attractive features of orchid flowers such as fragrance, colour and unusual shapes are not there for your benefit — their only role is to attract and in some cases capture a pollinator. This may be a bee, wasp, butterfly, moth, grub, fly, mosquito or humming bird. In most cases the attractions are tailor-made for a specific insect. The usual promise is food, but there is no pollen available as it is all wrapped up in waxy balls (pollinia) which is for reproduction only. The insect must be induced to go to the column to pick up a pollinium on its back and then pass it on to the stigma of the next flower. Orchids have evolved various ways to attract a suitable pollinator, and these are described below.

MIMICRY

Oncidium

Here the flower has evolved to look and sometimes smell like the pollinator or other insect — the magnetism is either sex or anger. Sex first. Here the flower looks like a female bee or wasp, and is open before the true females emerge. Males are attracted and the flower is pollinated as mating is attempted — examples are *Trichocerus* and *Ophrys*. The attraction in other cases is anger. With *Oncidium* the flower head looks like a swarm of bees as it flutters in the breeze — the flowers are attacked by a bee flying by and pollination takes place.

FRAGRANCE

It is usual to say that most orchids are not fragrant, but we must be careful here. Some emit odours which cannot be detected by humans — these may be pheromones which promise sex rather than food. Fragrance may only be produced at certain times — night time for nocturnal moths, bright sunny days for butterflies and so on. Fragrance is usually very slight or absent from hybrids of sweet-smelling species.

COLOUR

All the colours can be found, except true black, and they usually play an important role. Day-flying insects require bright colours, and the lip is often unusually colourful. The situation is different with orchids fertilized by night flyers such as moths — a clear outline is needed and so white or pastel shades are the predominant colours.

CAPTURE

Paphiopedilum

Capture is perhaps the most spectacular of all the techniques. With the Slipper Orchids such as *Paphiopedilum* the pollinator is attracted by a faint odour and falls into the pouch. In order to get out it has to climb up step-like hairs and must pass the column to reach the exit. The most sophisticated technique is found in *Coryanthes* — here the bee is intoxicated by chemicals on the edge of the bucket-like lip. It falls into the water below and has to climb out to dry, but not before passing the reproductive organs on the column.

CHAPTER 2

CHOOSING & BUYING

There is probably no reason for you to read this chapter if you are an experienced orchid grower, but it is vital for you to do so if you are a beginner or a complete novice. Choosing the wrong orchids or buying poor specimens can lead to early death, and you may well end up with your original thought that "orchids are just too difficult".

They are not. There are many which are really easy to grow in the home as well as others which offer a real challenge in the greenhouse. The first step is to follow a few simple rules at the choosing and buying stages.

CHOOSING

You want to buy an orchid. Ask yourself the following five questions — the plant you have in mind should not be ruled out by any of the answers.

QUESTION 1 : WHERE WILL IT HAVE TO LIVE?

Some orchids can thrive in the limited light and relatively dry air in the average room — others need the light and moist air in a greenhouse. Read the appropriate sections in Chapters 9 and 11 to check if the orchid is suitable.

QUESTION 2 : HOW LOW WILL THE TEMPERATURE FALL IN WINTER?

This is a vital question. The winter temperature requirement may be Cool (50°-55°F, 10°-13°C), Intermediate (55°-60°F, 13°-16°C) or Warm (over 60°F, 16°C). A centrally-heated living room will provide a Warm environment and an unheated room will be Cool or Intermediate, but for an accurate assessment you should use a maximum/minimum thermometer during a cold winter spell. Orchids will generally tolerate short periods which are somewhat higher or lower than these ranges, and the 'Easy' group (see Question 5) are even more tolerant, but it would be foolhardy to try to grow a Cool-type orchid under Warm conditions, and vice-versa. Check the orchid's temperature need in Chapter 11.

QUESTION 3 : HOW MUCH LIGHT WILL IT GET?

Another vital question. Some orchids need really bright surroundings and are unsuitable for room cultivation — others can cope with less light and can grow quite happily on a windowsill. Check the orchid's light need in Chapter 11.

QUESTION 4 : HOW MUCH SPACE IS AVAILABLE?

Space may be limited, as when growing orchids on a windowsill or under lights. You may pick an orchid which is far too tall when ordering from a catalogue or website. Always check the expected height if in doubt.

QUESTION 5 : HOW MUCH EXPERIENCE DO I HAVE?

If you are a beginner then choose your first plants from the list below, selecting ones with the temperature and light requirements which you can provide. You can then move to more difficult subjects as you gain experience.

The 'Easy' group

Brassavola	*Encyclia*
Brassia	*Epidendrum*
Cattleya	*Miltoniopsis*
Cambria	*Oncidium*
Cymbidium	*Paphiopedilum*
Dendrobium	*Phalaenopsis*

Choose a popular hybrid where available rather than a species

BUYING

MAKING A START

The usual starting point is to buy or be given a *Phalaenopsis* or *Paphiopedilum* — the popular hybrids are able to thrive in the limited light and the warmth of the average living room. The plant is kept for its long-lasting flower display and then is thrown away like Cyclamen or Poinsettia. The next stage is to try your hand with other easy ones which are readily available — try a miniature *Cymbidium* if the room is unheated. Remember that hybrids are usually easier than species.

The next step is to induce the plant to flower again once the first flush has died. This makes you an orchid grower rather than just an orchid keeper, and you will need to know the rules for orchid care (Chapter 3) and after some time the way to repot (Chapter 4). A greenhouse is the next stage, and now you can grow a much larger selection. You may well have been bitten by the orchid bug, and you might try propagation, hybridisation and exhibiting. Now you are an orchid hobbyist.

But we are running ahead of ourselves. Your first job is to buy an orchid or two, and there are several types of source from which to make your choice — see overleaf.

WHAT TO LOOK FOR

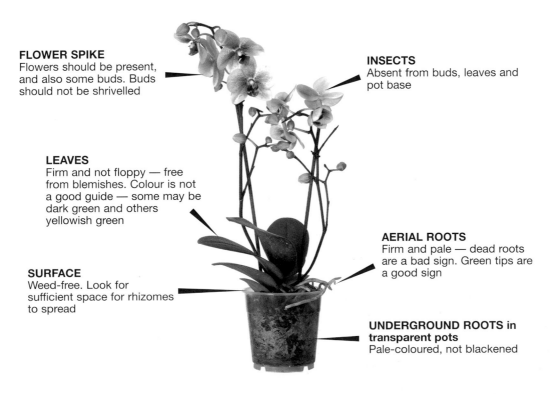

FLOWER SPIKE
Flowers should be present, and also some buds. Buds should not be shrivelled

INSECTS
Absent from buds, leaves and pot base

LEAVES
Firm and not floppy — free from blemishes. Colour is not a good guide — some may be dark green and others yellowish green

AERIAL ROOTS
Firm and pale — dead roots are a bad sign. Green tips are a good sign

SURFACE
Weed-free. Look for sufficient space for rhizomes to spread

UNDERGROUND ROOTS in transparent pots
Pale-coloured, not blackened

WHERE TO BUY ORCHIDS

STORE

Nearly all orchids are bought over the counter at a garden centre, florist, supermarket, DIY superstore or department store. The great advantage is that a source of supply is on your doorstep, and you can see what you are getting. Without these outlets the growing of orchids would still be a specialist hobby, so we should be grateful. There are, however, disadvantages. The range on offer is strictly limited — in Britain the High St. orchids are

Cambria • *Cymbidium* • *Dendrobium*
Miltoniopsis • *Oncidium* • *Paphiopedilum*
Phalaenopsis

In larger outlets you may find a few others, such as *Zygopetalum*, but you cannot build up a varied collection using this as your sole source. Another disadvantage is the lack of information on the label.

Taking it home

Make sure the plant is properly wrapped before leaving the store or nursery — several sheets of newspaper will do. The purpose of this wrapping is twofold — to protect leaves and flowers from damage and to keep out draughts. In winter the protecting cover should be closed at the top.

The danger of prolonged exposure to cold air during the walk to the car is obvious, but just as much damage can be done by putting plants in the boot of the car in the height of summer.

Moving from a bright greenhouse at the nursery to the relatively subdued light in a room calls for a period of acclimatisation. For a couple of weeks keep it out of direct sunlight and do not give it too much heat or water.

NURSERY

The drawback here is obvious — you may have to drive many miles to get to your nearest nursery. But the advantages are equally obvious — there will be a large and varied selection from which to choose and also detailed information from knowledgeable people. You can buy plants 'in spike', of course, with buds and flowers, but you can also buy smaller immature plants or seedlings. These call for patience as you may have to wait months or years for blooms, but you save money. Going to an orchid show to buy your stock is a good idea — a number of suppliers will be there and advice is readily available.

CATALOGUE

This is the traditional way of shopping for orchids once you have passed the store stage. You are spared the chore of bringing it home and the range on offer allows you to build up a varied collection. Descriptions are often sketchy, but the supplier is only a telephone call away.

ON LINE

The internet is an advance on the catalogue as it brings the nursery to you. The information on the web pages is up-to-date and there are usually abundant photographs and guidance notes. Ordering on line is quick and easy. With the internet you have access to the world's nurseries, but do take care if you are thinking of buying orchids from an overseas source. Buying from a nursery outside the European Union calls for permission and health certificates which cost time and money.

ORCHID NURSERIES

United Kingdom

The orchids you buy in British garden centres, DIY superstores etc have been grown in Continental Europe. There are very few commercial orchid growers in the United Kingdom, and they cater for the more serious orchid enthusiast who wants named out-of-the-ordinary types. Nearly all issue catalogues and have websites, but visits are usually by appointment. Some exhibit at orchid shows and are an excellent source of both plants and information.

NURSERY	ADDRESS	TELEPHONE & WEBSITE	CATALOGUE AVAILABLE	SUNDRIES AVAILABLE	OPEN TO VISITORS
BURNHAM NURSERIES LTD	Forches Cross Newton Abbot Devon TQ12 6PZ	01626 352233 www.orchids.uk.com	Yes	Yes	Yes
DAVID STEAD ORCHIDS	Greenscapes Horticultural Centre Brandon Crescent Shadwell Leeds LS17 9JH	0113 2893933 www.davidsteadorchids.co.uk	Yes	Yes	Yes, by appointment
EQUATORIAL PLANT CO	Gray Lane Barnard Castle Co Durham DL12 8PD	01833 690519 www.equatorialplants.com	Yes		Yes, by appointment
LAURENCE HOBBS ORCHIDS LTD	Bailiffs Cottage Nursery Hophurst Lane Crawley Down West Sussex RH10 4LN	01342 715142	Yes, Colour (£2.00) and Black & white	Yes	Yes, by appointment
McBEAN'S ORCHIDS	Resting Oak Hill Cooksbridge Lewes BN8 4PR	01273 400228 www.mcbeansorchids.co.uk	Yes	Yes	Yes
ORCHIDS by PETER WHITE	61 Stanwell Lea Middleton Cheney Banbury Oxon OX17 2RF	01295 712159 www.orchidsbypeterwhite.co.uk	Price list only	Yes	Yes, by appointment
PLESTED ORCHIDS	38 Florence Road College Town Sandhurst Berks GU47 0QD	01276 32947 www.plestedorchids.com	Yes	Yes	Yes, by appointment
RATCLIFFE ORCHIDS LTD	Pitcot Lane Owslebury Winchester Hampshire SO21 1LR	01962 777372 www.ratcliffe.uk.com	Yes	Yes	On advertised dates, by appointment

United States

Hundreds of orchid nurseries are spread throughout the mainland and in Hawaii. Catalogues are often colourful and many have excellent websites — visitors are generally welcome. Unfortunately, hardly any of them export to Europe because of the need for CITES permits (see page 55) and plant health certificates. A few do send flasks (page 43) overseas as these are not covered by these restrictions. The American Orchid Society issues an Orchid Source Directory to its members.

CHAPTER 3

ORCHID CARE

As with any pot plant the orchid you have bought needs light, water, food and a certain amount of winter warmth. Some are tolerant of a wide range of conditions — these belong to the easy group which fit in well with the average greenhouse and home environment. Others have highly specific needs which may be demanding — these are the difficult ones. So not all orchids need the same type of care, but all have certain basic requirements which differ from the way we care for other pot plants.

The main reason for this is that their roots are different (see page 6) and as a result cannot be grown in ordinary soil or compost. Orchid compost contains little or no food reserves and so regular feeding is necessary — orchid roots soon rot if kept waterlogged and so overwatering must be avoided. Many orchids are less tolerant of dry air than other pot plants but they are more tolerant of failure to water on time — nearly all have water-holding pseudobulbs.

Forget the idea that orchids are hot house plants which need constantly high temperatures. Few like warm nights and some benefit from being stood outdoors in summer. The popular 'house plant' orchids such as the Moth Orchid are easier to grow in a centrally-heated room than most other indoor plants.

The secret of orchid green fingers is to keep things in balance. When the room or greenhouse is warmer than usual then watering, air humidity and ventilation need to be increased. Reduced light calls for less warmth, and a resting plant requires less water and little or no feeding.

The death of an orchid is always sad and can be expensive. There are many possible causes. Listed below are the most common ones — the Seven Deadly Sins of orchid care.

The Seven Deadly Sins

TOO MUCH FERTILIZER
Two rules — do not feed when plants are not actively growing and do not exceed the recommended dose

DIRECT RADIANT HEAT
Orchids should never be placed in front of a radiator. Too much heat leads to leaf collapse

WET LEAVES
Leaves which are left wet overnight are a common cause of fatal disease. Water and mist early in the day

OVERWATERING
The main cause of death. Follow the watering rules — do not assume lack of water is the cause of all ills

COLD DRAUGHTS
Draughts are not the same as ventilation. Draughts involve the rapid movement of air between one opening and another

DRY & STUFFY AIR
Some method of increasing air moisture is needed for most orchids and so is air movement around the plant

STRONG SUMMER SUN
Too much sunlight leads to scorching heat. Some direct sun may be recommended, but shade from midday summer sun is always required

Give them the TEMPERATURE they need

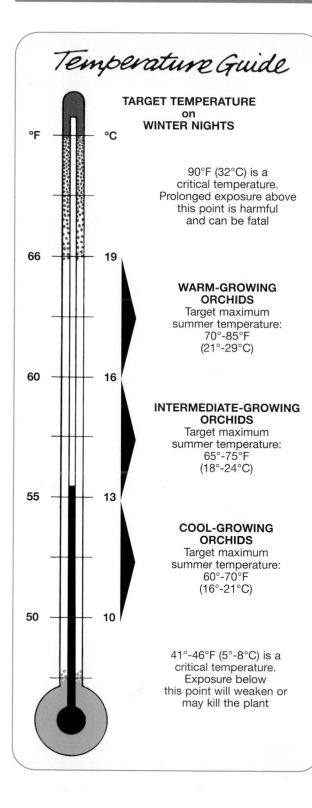

Temperature Guide

TARGET TEMPERATURE on WINTER NIGHTS

90°F (32°C) is a critical temperature. Prolonged exposure above this point is harmful and can be fatal

°F — °C

66 — 19

WARM-GROWING ORCHIDS
Target maximum summer temperature:
70°-85°F
(21°-29°C)

60 — 16

INTERMEDIATE-GROWING ORCHIDS
Target maximum summer temperature:
65°-75°F
(18°-24°C)

55 — 13

COOL-GROWING ORCHIDS
Target maximum summer temperature:
60°-70°F
(16°-21°C)

50 — 10

41°-46°F (5°-8°C) is a critical temperature. Exposure below this point will weaken or may kill the plant

There are two golden rules:

- Try to buy orchids with a winter temperature range which they can expect to find in their new home.

- Most orchids need at least a 10°F (5°C) difference between the day and night temperatures.

Orchids are divided into three groups based on their requirement for warmth — there are Cool-, Intermediate- and Warm-growing types. The winter minimums and the summer maximums are shown on the left, but you should not try to follow these figures slavishly. Some day-to-day variation is actually beneficial, some genera span two of the groups, and these groupings are based on species and not on hybrids which are generally more tolerant of variations.

An orchid in the home must cope with the temperature range in the room — warmth is set for human comfort and not for plants. We therefore choose Cool-loving types such as *Odontoglossum* or *Miltoniopsis* for rooms which receive little heat and *Phalaenopsis* for areas with central heating. We can still take some action to widen the range — Cool-growing types such as *Cymbidium* can be kept in the living room for most of the year and then moved to an unheated room for winter. Warm- or Intermediate-growing orchids can be moved off windowsills and into the room to avoid winter chills. Do not draw curtains to enclose orchids on the windowsill in winter.

The situation is different in the greenhouse. We can set the thermostat to suit our collection — a winter minimum of 55°-60°F (13°-16°C) will suit a large number of orchids. A large greenhouse can, of course, be divided up to provide two different environments, and even a small greenhouse will have a warmer and cooler area — remember that the roof area will be warmer than a low bench.

COOL-GROWING ORCHIDS

Some form of heater is required to maintain a minimum temperature of 50°F (10°C) during the depths of winter — this heating period usually lasts from early October to early May. An occasional drop to 45°F (7°C) for short periods should do no harm, but it is even more important here to make sure that the compost is not kept wet. Examples include *Cymbidium*, *Dendrobium*, *Odontoglossum*, *Miltoniopsis*, *Coelogyne* and *Masdevallia*. Some Intermediate types such as *Encyclia* and *Zygopetalum* can cope with Cool conditions.

Cymbidium

INTERMEDIATE-GROWING ORCHIDS

Heating may be needed from September to early June — compared to a Cool house two or three times more fuel will be required. Most of the orchids listed in this book can be grown under Intermediate conditions. Examples include *Cattleya*, *Oncidium*, *Encyclia*, *Zygopetalum*, Cambria, *Paphiopedilum*, *Epidendrum* and *Angraecum*. Some can be housed under Cool or Warm conditions — see the lists above and below.

Zygopetalum

WARM-GROWING ORCHIDS

A source of heat will be required nearly all year round to ensure that the night temperature does not fall below 60°F (16°C). A major problem is how to maintain a high enough relative humidity for types which need moist air — see page 22. There are two popular orchids which need a minimum temperature of 65°F (18°C) and do not like cooler conditions — *Vanda* and *Phalaenopsis*. Many Intermediate types, however, can grow successfully in warm conditions — examples include *Angraecum*, *Neofinetia* and *Rhynchostylis*.

Phalaenopsis

KEEPING THE HEAT DOWN UNDER GLASS

In late spring and summer the temperature has to be reduced to keep the plants below the overheating level. Dry heat is more dangerous than moist heat, and several interlinked methods can be used to lower the temperature. Damping down the floor (see page 22) and misting the plants will help, coupled with adequate ventilation. As soon as the temperature continually remains above 77°F (25°C) it is essential to apply some form of sun screen. Blinds or proprietary shading paint is the usual answer. Do not use lime wash as it is difficult to remove in autumn.

KEEPING AN EYE ON THE TEMPERATURE

A maximum-minimum thermometer is an essential piece of equipment if you want to take orchid growing seriously. This will tell you not only the current temperature but also the highest and lowest temperature since the instrument was last set. The traditional type is a mercury-filled U-tube, but the pointer-and-finger type which was easier to read came along, and now there is the digital type which is reset by the touch of a button. You will need two in the greenhouse so that you can spot the variation between both ends — always place the instrument away from direct sunlight.

Give them the LIGHT they need

Correct lighting is more than just a matter of giving a plant the brightness it needs — there are two distinct aspects which control growth. The **duration** required is the same for most types — there must be 12-16 hours of light to maintain active growth. Less will slow down food production — more can inhibit flower production.

The light **intensity** requirement is generally high compared to the average pot plant, but it can vary quite widely from one orchid type to another, as shown on the next page. Occasionally an orchid is left to scorch on an unshaded sunny windowsill, but most plants in the home receive too little rather than too much light. For many varieties the best summer location is an east-facing windowsill or a south-facing one which is shielded by net curtains. A west-facing windowsill is less satisfactory and a north-facing one is not suitable for orchids. In winter the plants should be moved to the brightest spot available.

In the greenhouse some form of shading is necessary in late spring and summer. This has the dual effect of lowering both the temperature and light intensity — see page 17.

- It is necessary to turn the pot occasionally to prevent lop-sided growth — make only a slight turn each time. Do not turn the plant when it is in bud.

- Do not move a plant suddenly from a shady spot to a sunny location. Acclimatise for a few days by moving to a brighter spot each day.

- Keep glass and plants clean in winter — removing dust can increase light intensity by up to 10 per cent.

- White or cream-coloured walls and ceiling improve plant growth and flowering by reflecting light in a room where lighting may be inadequate.

- The correct duration of light exposure depends on the orchid type and season. In general terms it is 12-16 hours as stated on the left, but there are several points to consider. Do not expose to more than 16 hours of light, but an orchid which is not resting needs about 14 hours of light in winter. Some orchids such as *Oncidium* and *Dendrobium* will not bloom if there is not a period of darkness during the night — even a table lamp can be a problem if left on all the time.

ORCHIDS UNDER LIGHTS

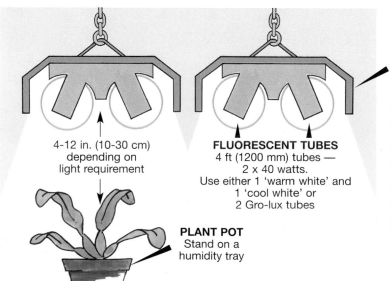

4-12 in. (10-30 cm) depending on light requirement

FLUORESCENT TUBES
4 ft (1200 mm) tubes — 2 x 40 watts.
Use either 1 'warm white' and 1 'cool white' or 2 Gro-lux tubes

PLANT POT
Stand on a humidity tray

REFLECTOR
Used to direct light downwards on to the plants and away from the eyes of the viewer

Growing under lights adds a new dimension — you and not nature are in full control of the duration and intensity of the light. Leave on for 14-16 hours and stand the plants on a humidity tray. Choose from the average- and lowest-light requirement list — compact varieties are the most suitable.

HIGHEST LIGHT REQUIREMENT

These orchids are not for the windowsill nor for growing under fluorescent lights — these sun-seekers need a greenhouse in an open situation. Despite this requirement for very bright conditions, it is still necessary to provide some shade against summer sun. Examples include *Vanda* species and some *Cymbidium*, *Dendrobium* and *Laelia* species and hybrids. As a general rule orchids with thick, leathery leaves need more light than those with soft and/or fleshy leaves. Some orchid genera will thrive in either high or average brightness — see below.

Vanda

AVERAGE LIGHT REQUIREMENT

These orchids will thrive on an east-facing windowsill, a summer-shaded greenhouse or under fluorescent lights — see previous page. Most orchids belong here — *Miltoniopsis*, *Brassia*, *Cattleya*, *Cymbidium* hybrids, Cambria and *Coelogyne* are examples. *Oncidium*, *Brassavola* and *Phragmipedium* are examples of orchids which can be kept in an average or high light location. These orchids need shade from the sun during the brightest part of the day between late spring and autumn, but require unshaded bright light in winter.

Miltoniopsis

LOWEST LIGHT REQUIREMENT

These orchids need to be kept away from direct sunlight from spring to autumn. They will thrive on a shaded east-facing windowsill or close to a west-facing windowsill, or you can house them under a couple of fluorescent lights. The classic 'low light' orchids are *Phalaenopsis* species and hybrids, and the non strap-leaved *Paphiopedilum* species and hybrids. Other orchids in this group include *Ludisia* and *Masdevallia*. Only a few orchids will flourish in low light, but many other pot plants can thrive at this light intensity.

Paphiopedilum

LOOK AT THE LEAVES

TOO MUCH LIGHT
Paler than normal.
Yellow or pink cast present.
Severe sunburn results in brown or black patches.
Petal edges may be discoloured.

CORRECT LIGHT
Usually mid-green.
Flowers normal.
Pseudobulbs normal.

TOO LITTLE LIGHT
Darker than normal.
Surface is dull and width is narrower than usual.
Flowers may be few or absent.
Pseudobulbs are thin or shrivelled.

Give them the WATER they need

Watering Guide

◄ **DRY IN WINTER orchids**
Many epiphytes need a resting period — give just enough water to prevent pseudobulb shrinkage. Examples are *Cattleya*, *Encyclia*, *Coelogyne* and *Brassia*

◄ **MOIST/DRY orchids**
The standard recommendation is to water thoroughly between spring and autumn, letting the top ½ in. (1 cm) dry out between waterings. Water more sparingly in winter — do not keep the medium constantly moist at this time. Examples include *Ludisia* and *Epidendrum*, and the Dry in Winter epiphytes during the growing season

◄ **MOIST AT ALL TIMES orchids**
Here the medium is kept moist but not wet at all times. Watering is more frequent than with the Moist/Dry group, but be careful to avoid waterlogging. Reduce the frequency in winter. The aim is evenly moist conditions. Examples are *Cymbidium*, *Miltoniopsis*, *Paphiopedilum*, *Phalaenopsis*, *Vanda* and Cambria

◄ **WET AT ALL TIMES orchids**
Very few orchids belong to this group. Water thoroughly and frequently to keep the medium wet. *Phragmipedium* is the only popular example

WATERING PROBLEMS

With serious overwatering and underwatering the symptoms are the same — yellowing leaves and shrivelled pseudobulbs. Carefully lift the plant out of the pot to find the culprit. White, firm roots indicate underwatering — soft, blackened roots reveal overwatering. A common cause of underwatering is the presence of massed rhizomes and roots on top of the medium of a pot-bound plant. Water cannot penetrate, so use the immersion method. Repot as soon as practical.

Without water an orchid must die. Because of this obvious fact many beginners give dribbles of water every day or two — the amount is increased when the leaves turn yellow and does not stop when winter arrives. The result is that the roots rot in the soggy airless mass — more plants are killed by overwatering than any other single cause.

Orchids take longer than nearly all other pot plants to show the effects of overwatering or underwatering, but they also take longer to recover once they are watered properly — recovery may take years. Learning how to water correctly is essential, but unfortunately it is not a matter of just one or two simple rules.

Each orchid has its own basic need for water — see the chart on the left and the information provided in the A-Z section. It is not possible to recommend a set time between waterings — it depends on the plant as already stated, and also several other factors described in the 'How often to water' section on the next page. The most usual time scale is about once or twice a week during the growing season and about once every two weeks in winter.

Plants with pseudobulbs need watering less frequently than other types, but the time comes when they will need watering or the pseudobulbs will shrink and the roots will be damaged. So how can you tell when it is time to water?

Moisture meters are available, but one of the best guides is to insert your forefinger in the medium up to the full depth of your fingernail. If the tip is dry when withdrawn then watering of the Moist at all Times group is necessary. With the Moist/Dry ones in large pots you can wait a day or two after this stage before watering. An alternative method is to feel the weight of the pot — with practice you can soon learn to tell when a pot has reached the ready-to-water stage.

HOW OFTEN TO WATER

You must never allow watering to become a regular routine whereby the pots are filled up every Sunday. The correct interval will vary greatly — the Watering Guide clearly shows that the gap may vary from a day or two to many weeks, depending on the orchid in question. The interval between waterings for an individual plant also varies with the season and changes in growing conditions.

THE PLANT

It has already been stressed that some orchids have either a rest period or complete dormancy in winter, so that little or no water is required. However, regular watering will be required when active growth is resumed in spring. The period between waterings is obviously longer for Moist/Dry orchids than Moist at all Times ones, but this first group must never dry out completely and the second group must not be constantly wet.

THE POT & MEDIUM

Clay pots dry out more quickly than plastic ones, but water is more evenly distributed in clay ones. Small pots need to be watered more often than large ones. The nature of the potting material also has an effect on the period between waterings — non-absorbent mineral materials such as rockwool require more frequent watering than absorbent organic materials such as sphagnum moss. Age is also a factor — old potting material retains water for a longer period than fresh compost.

THE ENVIRONMENT

As the temperature and light intensity increase, so does the need for water. The plant is growing more actively, which means more transpiration by the leaves and the higher warmth means more evaporation from the medium. An increase in evaporation and a resulting shortening of the watering interval also occur when the relative humidity falls (as in a centrally-heated room) or when the ventilation increases (as with a nearby open window).

THE WATER TO USE

Some people use water straight from the tap with no apparent ill effects, but this is safe only when the tap water is soft and the orchids are tough 'easy' ones. If your tap water is hard and high in minerals it will be necessary to water occasionally with soft mineral-free water — it is far better to use this soft water every time you water.

Both rainwater (provided it is not stagnant) and distilled water are suitable — a readily available and cheap alternative is water obtained from an ion-exchange kitchen filter. A word of warning — never use water which has been softened by the addition of sodium-based chemicals. One final point — water should be at room temperature before use.

THE WAY TO WATER

The **Watering can method** is the usual technique. Stand the pot in the sink or on the draining board and slowly pour water over the whole of the surface using a long-spouted watering can. Continue watering until water flows freely from the base, and leave to drain. Water in the morning, especially in winter.

The **Immersion method** is the preferred technique for pot-bound plants, orchids in baskets, slab displays and plants which have started to grow after a resting period. Immerse pots in water to just below the level of the medium and leave until the surface glistens. Allow to drain before returning to their growing quarters. Do not water newly-potted plants by the immersion method.

Give them the HUMIDITY they need

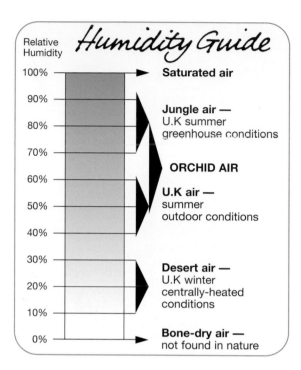

Humidity Guide

Relative Humidity	
100%	Saturated air
90%	
80%	Jungle air — U.K summer greenhouse conditions
70%	
60%	ORCHID AIR
50%	U.K air — summer outdoor conditions
40%	
30%	
20%	Desert air — U.K winter centrally-heated conditions
10%	
0%	Bone-dry air — not found in nature

Turning on a radiator or switching on the central heating in winter makes the room comfortable for you — but it can be distinctly uncomfortable for your orchid. The water vapour in the air is no longer sufficient to keep the atmosphere moist. The air becomes 'dry' — in technical terms the Relative Humidity has fallen. Orchids need moister air than nearly all other indoor and greenhouse plants, and so it is necessary to use one or more of the techniques described below to increase the moisture in the air around them. The Relative Humidity should be above 50%, but the specific requirement depends on the orchid you are growing. For 'easy' ones such as *Phalaenopsis* and *Paphiopedilum* an occasional misting plus a humidity tray are all that is required. At the other end of the scale a terrarium may be needed for the jungle air lovers — see page 57. Don't guess the Relative Humidity — buy a digital hygrometer.

MOISTURE-RAISING METHODS

MISTING

A support technique rather than a stand-alone one — the moisture-raising effect is short lived. Use a hand-held mister and spray the leaves — avoid the flowers if you can. Treat when the hygrometer tells you that the air is too dry. Misting is necessary for plants in baskets and for slab displays — mist the roots and leaves. A few precautions: To prevent leaf-spotting do not use tap water in a hard water area — to avoid botrytis attack do not mist in winter if the indoor temperature is low. Do not mist late in the day.

GROUPING

Plants brought together have the benefit of increased moisture arising from the damp compost surface and from the water transpired by the foliage. The moisture-raising effect is, of course, even greater when the pots are stood in a humidity tray.

DAMPING DOWN

In summer the floor and the benches in the greenhouse should be hosed down. As the water evaporates the temperature is lowered and air humidity is increased. In addition dry-air pests such as red spider mite and thrips are discouraged. Damp down in the morning. On hot days repeat in the early afternoon — do not damp down when the temperature is falling.

HUMIDITY TRAY

A simple and excellent method for increasing humidity around the plants. Any waterproof and rust-proof container which is at least 3 in. (7.5 cm) deep will do — fill to 1-2 in. (2.5-5 cm) with gravel or small pebbles. Add water and keep topped up so that half the gravel layer is under water. Wash the gravel every few months. As an alternative a raised rust-proof grill can be used to support the plants above the water in the tray.

Give them the FOOD they need

NITROGEN (N)	The *leaf maker* which promotes stem growth and foliage production. Needs to be balanced with some potash for orchids
PHOSPHATES (P_2O_5)	The *root maker* which stimulates active rooting in the medium. Necessary, but all compound fertilizers have sufficient
POTASH (K_2O)	The *flower maker* which hardens growth so that flowering is encouraged at the expense of leaf growth
TRACE ELEMENTS	Present in some house plant feeds — derived from organic or chemical sources. Shortage can cause leaf discoloration

The numbers which appear on the label are the ratios of the major nutrients. For example 20:12:12 tells you that the product contains 20% nitrogen, 12% phosphates and 12% potash. The nitrogen should not have been derived from urea.

Your orchid will need an adequate supply of nitrogen, phosphates and potash plus small amounts of trace elements in order to achieve its full growth and flowering potential. To provide this requirement you will have to use a fertilizer, but before buying a house plant food and following the instructions on the label there are two points to consider. First of all, never regard a fertilizer as a tonic to restore sick plants — a plant which is clearly unhealthy or not growing should not be fed. Secondly, orchids need less food than other pot plants — the instructions on the plant food bottle do not apply. The information below tells you what fertilizer to use and also when and how to use it. Follow the recommendations and do not overdose — too much fertilizer will result in blackened leaf tips and growth may be stunted. As with watering — a little less is better than a little too much.

WHAT TO BUY

Granules, powders, slow-release tablets, liquids — there is a wide range of types and strengths. The best choice is a soluble powder or liquid concentrate which is added to the water you use on your plants. You can pick an ordinary house plant fertilizer and use it at half strength, but it is better to buy a specific orchid fertilizer from a reputable supplier — these can be obtained by mail order from an orchid nursery. A general-purpose fertilizer with all the major nutrients in approximately equal amounts can be used whenever feeding is required, but experienced growers usually prefer to follow a two-feed plan. A high-nitrogen formulation is used in spring and summer to promote growth and this is later changed to a high-potash feed to stimulate flowering and pseudobulb ripening.

WHEN AND HOW TO FEED

With ordinary pot plants there is no need to feed for some time after potting — there are nutrients in the compost and these should provide sufficient food for 6-8 weeks. There are usually no nutrients in the medium in which your orchid is growing, and so you have to begin feeding right from the start. Growers use different feeding routines — the rule is to find one that works for you and then stick to it! A popular routine is to add fertilizer at every other watering. Use a watering can for water/fertilizer application — for a large collection of orchids a hose-end dilutor can be used to add the feed to the water. The procedure with slab displays is to take them down and dip them several times in a bowl of the fertilizer solution. Reduce or stop feeding in winter — check in the A-Z guide.

Give them the FRESH AIR they need

Plants, unlike pets, do not have to be provided with air to enable them to breathe. Green leaves manufacture oxygen, and so orchids may stay alive in a closed container. They may well succumb because of other factors, but it will not be shortage of oxygen. Despite this unique property, most orchids will suffer if they are not supplied with a gentle air current around the leaves — this air movement is usually supplied by opening a window, vent or door. There are five basic benefits:

• The temperature of the air is lowered.

• Water on the leaves evaporates more quickly — stagnant, muggy air is one of the main causes of disease in winter.

• Stems are strengthened.

• Traces of toxic vapours are removed.

• Cold and warm air are mixed together and more evenly distributed — especially important in winter.

Gentle air movement is required, but you must guard against draughts. These are air currents moving rapidly and directly across the plants. When the temperature outside is appreciably less than that of the room or greenhouse you should open nearby vents or windows not at all or do so only slightly. Ventilating the room is not enough for some orchids — some types such as *Cymbidium* should be stood outdoors in summer.

IN THE HOME

In a room the air around the plants may become stagnant. Tobacco smoke is not a problem and gas is no longer harmful to plants, but the smoke from an open fire and the fumes from wet paint can be damaging. The real problem is the lack of air movement — the situation is worst in a room with central heating. The answer is to create a gentle air current. As noted above you must avoid creating a strong draught across the leaves — the problem is heightened when two windows across from each other are opened. A small fan directed away from the plants is a great help when it is too hot or too cold to open the window — best of all is a slow-moving ceiling fan.

IN THE GREENHOUSE

Features to look for

Single roof vent makes opening into the wind occasionally unavoidable

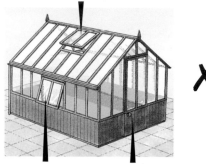

✗

Side vents are not a good idea

Hinged doors may not be easy to keep ajar

Vents on either side allow opening away from the wind at any time

Sliding doors can easily be kept open to any desired width

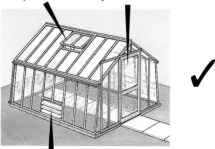

✓

Louvred floor-level vents allow controlled air movement

Opening the roof vent is the basic method for increasing ventilation. One or more may be open all day and night in midsummer or they may be raised very slightly for just part of the day in winter. Adequate ventilation is more important for orchids requiring Cool conditions than those which need Intermediate or Warm surroundings, but for all orchids you should never open the vents with abandon. It does refresh the atmosphere in the house and it lowers the temperature on hot days, but it also results in lowering the humidity. Damp down and mist the foliage when opening up the house in summer. Use the side vents with care — draughts across leaves are damaging. The door may be opened if necessary. Use a screen if insects are a problem. An electric fan blowing away from the plants is useful where opening the vents is undesirable.

Give them the REST they need

The purpose of pseudobulbs in nature is to enable the plants to draw on the reserves of water and nutrients which have been stored during the rainy season. As a result they are able to survive the annual period of drought. This is the resting period, and we must mimic it with some of our orchids if they are to thrive and continue to flower. We have to stop feeding and provide a reduced amount of water. This leaves us with a problem. The reduction in watering may range from none at all to the sort of reduced supply we would give to the average house plant, and to complicate matters further this resting period may last from a few weeks to several months. The period of complete or partial dormancy usually occurs in winter, but not always — several orchids rest in summer.

The A-Z guide provides information. You will see that there are some genera such as *Cymbidium* which do not become fully dormant, so watering has to be reduced and not stopped. Others like *Cattleya* and *Laelia* do become dormant, and here you must water only if severe shrivelling of the pseudobulbs occurs. The orchids which lose their leaves in winter tell you when to stop watering — examples include *Pleione*, *Bletilla* and the deciduous types of *Calanthe* and *Dendrobium*. With these plants stop watering at leaf fall and resume when new growth starts in the New Year.

Although the books will tell you which genera need a resting period, they cannot tell you just when to stop and when to start again — here you have to rely on the plant to tell you. At the start of the resting period growth ceases and the green on the tips of the aerial roots disappears. At the end of the resting period new growth appears at the base of the pseudobulb.

Evergreen orchids without pseudobulbs do not have a true resting period as they have no stored water. In general they require a reduction in the amount of water in winter — examples include *Phalaenopsis* and *Paphiopedilum*. The rule is to keep the potting medium moist but not waterlogged.

Laelia: a resting period of several weeks is necessary in winter

Phragmipedium: no resting period is required in winter

Give them the GROOMING they need

DEAD-HEADING

The general rule is to gently remove faded flowers before they drop, and to cut back the spike to just above the base when all the blooms have gone. *Phalaenopsis* is the exception, as a second spike will often appear if the spike is shortened rather than removed. See page 108 for details.

TRIMMING

Old leaves may turn brown or their tips may be blackened. Remove any dead foliage with their stalks. Unsightly ends should be cut off by using really sharp scissors — try to create an outline which preserves the natural leaf shape.

CLEANING

An unsightly deposit may develop on the surface of the leaves for two reasons. In the home a layer of dust may settle which blocks the leaf pores and forms a light-reducing screen apart from spoiling the appearance of large- or decorative-leaved varieties. Regular misting will help to reduce this problem, but in a hard water area it can have a disfiguring effect which is even worse than the coating of dust — white chalky spots over the leaf surface. To remove the spots you can gently sponge the foliage with tepid water which has been softened through an ion-exchange kitchen filter. Remove dust with a soft cloth and support the leaf with your hand — rub gently with a moist paper towel. Some growers prefer to use milk.

STAKING

The purpose of staking the flower spike is to ensure that the flower head is properly supported and the blooms are able to put their best face forward.

The golden rule for orchids which bear numerous flowers in sprays or along arching stems is to begin early — *Phalaenopsis* is the best example. Many types of stakes are available — there are metal ones for pushing into the medium or clipping on to the pot, but the most popular stake is the green split bamboo cane. Stake at the early bud stage. The cane should be pushed into the medium close to the spike when it is about 6 in. (15 cm) high. Twist and turn the cane as you push downwards in order to do as little root damage as possible. Attach the spike to the cane with twist-ties or raffia — do not tie too tightly. Put the first tie about 2 in. (5 cm) above the base and the top one about 2 in. (5 cm) below the lowermost bud. Always replace the pot after watering in the same position with regard to light — you can put it somewhere else once the blooms are open.

The time for staking orchids which bear one or two flowers on top of the spike is when the bud is swollen but before it has opened.

CHAPTER 4
POTS & POTTING

You cannot avoid the task of repotting if you are to take orchid growing seriously — the reason is that all the plants in pots in your collection will require a change of their growing medium at some time.

Right from the start you will see that the materials and procedures are different to the ones which are used for repotting ordinary pot plants. For aspidistras and azaleas you have the choice of a clay or plastic pot and a wide selection of potting composts available from your local garden store. These composts are dense with good water- and nutrient-holding properties — a reservoir is provided for the root hairs. The requirements for orchids are different, and you can see the reason on the next page. The hairless roots are covered with a water-holding layer — this means that many orchids can be grown in little or no compost if the roots are kept watered at frequent intervals. As a result the range of containers is wider than for the aspidistras and azaleas as supports which allow roots to hang in the air are available.

The composts are also different from the organic potting mixes used for ordinary pot plants — orchid composts are coarse and much more open. Another big difference — windowsill gardeners with a pot or two and the keen growers with a large and varied collection of house and conservatory plants choose from the same range of composts. With orchids the windowsill gardeners tend to go to their local garden centre for the only all-purpose orchid compost they stock. Not so the serious grower with a variety of orchids — composts are bought from an orchid nursery. Ready-made mixes are available, but many people prefer to buy ingredients and make their own blend or follow one of the many recipes which are available — see page 31.

So there are containers and composts which are not used for other plants, and there are also some aspects of the potting process which are unique to orchids. On the following pages you will find enough to make a start in this vital aspect of growing orchids.

CONTAINERS

Orchids are generally grown in pots, and the ones at the garden centre or DIY superstore are made of plastic. Clay or plastic pots have advantages and disadvantages, and both have their disciples. Wash used pots thoroughly before re-use. You cannot choose any size of container when you plan to repot. There are strict rules — see page 33.

CLAY POT

Traditional 'natural' appearance — compared to plastic pots they are less likely to topple over and there is less chance of waterlogging. There is a cooling effect as water evaporates from the sides. Choose a broad-based pot for a top-heavy plant.

PLASTIC POT

Various shapes and colours available — compared to clay pots they do not absorb potentially harmful salts from the water and they need less frequent watering. Roots clinging to the sides of the pot are not a problem at repotting time.

SEE-THROUGH POT

Pots made from semi-transparent plastic rather than the more usual opaque type offer a distinct advantage. Both roots and compost can be watched. Root rot due to overwatering can be seen, and so can loss of compost structure.

ORCHID POT

Pots specially made for orchids with extra drainage holes at the bottom and sides. Used to be popular, but it is now known that adding a layer of crock material, such as polystyrene chips, to an ordinary pot makes these special pots unnecessary.

SLATTED BASKET

Some orchids which rely on aerial roots (e.g *Vanda*) or have long pendent flower heads need an open-sided hanging container. A wooden slatted basket is the usual answer — line with sphagnum moss before filling with the potting medium.

SLAB DISPLAY

A piece of cork bark, tree branch, tree-fern fibre etc to which a suitable epiphyte is wired. The only medium used is sphagnum moss behind the plant — see page 31 for details. Like the slatted basket it is suited to the greenhouse and not the living room.

POT HOLDERS

A decorative pot holder (cachepot) can be used to house the pot, provided it is waterproof and large enough for the pot to be lifted out without difficulty for watering. Never water the pot when it is in its pot holder.

MIXED DISPLAYS

Various orchids with or without other house plants which have similar light and heat requirements can be grown together in a container for a mixed display, but each one should be kept in its own pot.

POTTING MEDIUMS

An orchid potting medium is more open and freer-draining than ordinary potting composts, and it is also less rich in nutrients — a few shop-bought mixtures contain added fertilizers but they are the exception. Soil is not used in the cultivation of epiphytic orchids. The orchid medium consists of one or more base ingredients which provide the essential properties listed above — in addition they must break down very slowly or not at all, and should have some water-holding capacity. There are a limited number in common use and the potting mediums they make fall into two groups — composts and inorganic mediums.

- **Composts** are potting mediums in which the base ingredient(s) is organic, being derived from living or dead plant material. The choice these days is generally between bark and coarse peat. In the past a variety of materials have been used, but are no longer popular due to scarcity, limited success, etc. Examples are tree-fern fibre, osmunda fibre and crushed cork. Composts do slowly break down, which calls for repotting at intervals — see page 32.

- **Inorganic mediums** are potting mediums in which the base ingredient is natural or synthetic, being derived from material which is not organic. Examples include horticultural foam and expanded clay pellets (aggregates), but the only one which is widely used is rockwool.

BASE MATERIALS

BARK

In the U.S fir bark is the standard base — in the U.K the choice is pine bark with or without the addition of coarse peat. Redwood bark has the advantage of breaking down very slowly, but it is in short supply. Do not confuse these orchid bark chips with bark chippings used for mulching. The bark used for growing orchids is available in three grades — fine (under ¼ in./0.5 cm) for seedling composts, medium (¼-1 in./0.5-2.5 cm) for standard orchid mixes, and coarse (over 1 in./2.5 cm) for compost specifically designed for thick rooted orchids such as *Vanda*. The water-holding capacity of bark is rather low, and so it is usual to add a material which will increase the reservoir effect — perlite, clay pellets and coarse peat are examples. Do not mix bark with rockwool. Before using bark it is wise to sift out the dust.

COARSE PEAT

A coarse grade of peat is used — garden-grade peat is too fine. Suitable for some fine-rooted types such as the Slipper Orchids but it is not open enough for most orchids — perlite, clay pellets and/or bark are needed in the mix.

ROCKWOOL

Not popular. Available in 1 cm or 2 cm cubes. Never breaks down, and overwatering is not a problem. No fertilizer-holding capacity, however, and is better used as an ingredient rather than a base material. Gloves needed when handling.

OPTIONAL EXTRAS

COIR

This waste coconut fibre holds water and is slow to break down, but it is not as free-draining as bark. Coir is sometimes used as the sole potting material, but it is more often used as an added ingredient to improve water-holding capacity.

PERLITE

A popular lightweight rock-based product — it has excellent water-holding and aerating properties and it does not readily decay. It is too water retentive for use as a base ingredient — use it by adding to bark or peat. Avoid the fine dust.

HYDROLECA

Unlike perlite these expanded clay pellets are heavy. They are porous with good water- and air-holding properties, but they are generally used with peat or bark in a mixture rather than as a base material. Useful when potting top-heavy plants.

SPHAGNUM MOSS

Live sphagnum moss was once an important base material but it is now less widely used. It generally holds too much water to be used on its own, but dry sphagnum moss moistened before use is often used to improve bark mixes.

CHARCOAL

The charcoal from hardwood trees is sometimes added as a 'sweetener' to the potting mix. It holds neither air nor water and provides no nutrients, but it does absorb undesirable acidic pollutants. Do not use if the water in your area is hard.

POLYSTYRENE

Polystyrene chips are light-weight and have excellent water- and air-holding properties. They do not break down and are inexpensive. A good additive for bark composts — one of the best materials for the crock layer in the pot. Do not mix with coarse peat.

POTTING MIXTURES

Shop-bought, nursery-made and home-made potting mixtures in the U.S are usually based on fir bark with the addition of materials to help the physical structure. In Britain the shop-bought mixes are based on coarse peat with or without bark plus a small amount of fertilizer, and the mixes offered by orchid nurseries are based on pine bark, coarse peat or sphagnum moss to which other materials such as perlite are added.

Experienced growers like to mix their own, and there is no 'right' formula for all orchids. *Phalaenopsis* favours bark in the compost, *Vanda* needs a more open compost than most other orchids, and so on. All sorts of combinations are used and recommended, but at first it is best to stick to a simple standard mix such as the one below:

Standard mix	6 parts bark (medium grade) 1 part perlite 1 part charcoal
Fine mix for seedlings and fine-rooted plants	4 parts bark (fine grade) 1 part perlite 1 part charcoal

The situation is different for terrestrial orchids. Some people use a standard mix such as the one above, but many growers prefer to use a soil-based mix. As an example:

1 part sterilized loam
1 part sharp sand
1 part coarse peat

MAKING A SLAB DISPLAY

Attach a suitable hanger to the back of the slab (bark, driftwood, tree branch etc) and staple a clump of damp sphagnum moss to it. Place the orchid on this pad and spread the roots outwards. Wrap fishing line or plastic-coated wire around the top and bottom of the moss pad to hold the orchid in place — the crown should face downwards. Mist regularly and water occasionally for 6 weeks and keep out of sunlight. After this period spray thoroughly or immerse in tepid water at weekly intervals.

POTTING

Repotting an orchid is not difficult, but you will have to forget the rules for transplanting ordinary pot plants. Here you will usually have to break up the compost ball to free the roots, and there will be no need to ensure that all the roots are in intimate contact with the medium. There are two separate potting systems:

- **Repotting** is usually carried out every couple of years — see below for details on timing. All spent compost and blackened roots are removed and the plant is then transferred to a pot which is a little larger than the previous one. Fresh compost is used to hold the orchid in its new home. This is the right time to divide the rhizomes to increase your stock — see page 35.

- **Dropping on** is carried out with seedlings and rooted cuttings at 6-monthly intervals in spring and autumn. The compost ball is not disturbed unless the medium has decayed — the plant is moved to a pot which is a little larger.

THE REASON TO REPOT

- The orchid has outgrown the container — rhizomes over the edges and/or plant pushing out of the container.

- The compost has decayed — it is time to repot when bark compost has become soil-like and drainage is poor.

- The plant has been damaged by overwatering.

THE TIME TO REPOT

- The recommended time is when new growth appears. This will be seen at the tips of the rhizomes — the new roots should not be more than 1 in. (2.5 cm) long.

- This new growth usually coincides with the end of the flowering season.

- Spring is the ideal season of the year.

GETTING READY TO REPOT

CROCKING MATERIAL
Broken clay pots, polystyrene chips or pebbles

WASTE BIN
A necessary item for the collection of rubbish

KNIFE
A necessary item for removing back bulbs, dividing rhizomes etc

POTS

SECATEURS

POTTING MIX

STERILISER
Tools must be sterilised between each repotting operation. Use a kitchen blow torch, cigarette lighter or immersion in methylated spirits (denatured alcohol)

NEWSPAPER
Spread out sheets of newspaper — work on the top sheet and remove with discarded material when repotting is finished. Repeat with each plant

ADDITIONAL ITEMS
Stakes and ties are necessary if the plant is large

Gloves are necessary if you are using rockwool

THE WAY TO REPOT

BEFORE YOU START
Choose a suitable pot — it should allow 2 years' growth but must be no more than 2 in. (5 cm) wider than the old one. *Phalaenopsis* is sometimes put back in the same pot. Water the plant the night before. Make sure that the medium is moist but not soggy.

STEP 2: Get the plant ready
Lay the pot on its side and gently pull out the plant. Run a knife around the compost ball if it refuses to move. Try again — if all else fails break or cut open the pot. Shake the plant so that all the decayed and loose potting medium falls away. Cut away dark and damaged roots — the healthy paler ones will have to be shortened if they are too long to fit into the pot without requiring bending. Do not cut back thick aerial roots which were growing outside the old pot — to bury these in potting medium would kill them. The final step is to remove some of the back bulbs if necessary — pseudobulbs in leaf should outnumber inactive ones.

STEP 5: Stake if necessary
Top-heavy orchids and ones with a sparse root system will need staking. Various metal types are available but a split bamboo cane pushed to the base of the pot is quite satisfactory. Attach the stem or stems to the cane with plant ties, raffia or garden twine.

STEP 4: Add potting medium
Add handfuls of the medium around the roots without moving the plant. Firm down gently with fingers and thumb or a blunt stick — after each couple of handfuls tap the pot on the bench to settle the plant. Continue until the bottom of the rhizome is ½-1 in. (1-2.5 cm) below the rim and its base is resting on the medium. Never cover the rhizome of a sympodial orchid or the crown of a monopodial one.

STEP 3: Hold the plant in position
Put a handful or two of the medium into the pot and hold the plant so that the bottom of the rhizome is a little below the rim. The oldest back bulb should be almost touching the inside of the pot and the growing tip should point to the furthest side. A monopodial orchid such as *Phalaenopsis* should be held in the centre of the pot.

STEP 1: Get the pot ready
Soak overnight if it is porous. Put a layer of crocking material to fill the bottom quarter of the pot. Broken fragments of clay pots are the traditional material, but polystyrene chips are better. Coarse gravel or small pebbles can be used if the plant is top-heavy and the pot is light. Cover the crocking matter with a thin layer of the potting medium.

AFTER YOU FINISH
Attach a label so that you will not forget the name of the orchid. Keep the pot away from bright light and water sparingly, but mist daily for 2-3 weeks. After this time the plant can be returned to its previous location and the watering and feeding routine restored.

CHAPTER 5
INCREASING YOUR STOCK

The differences between orchids and other pot plants are highlighted on numerous pages in this book — the unique flower anatomy, the unique root structure and so on. Propagation is yet another feature which demonstrates the extraordinary nature of the orchid. The basic ways by which we produce new stock from indoor plants are by taking stem cuttings and by sowing seed. With orchids the ability to propagate by means of stem cuttings is restricted to a relatively small number of genera, and the sowing of seed is out of the question for the ordinary gardener. Even growing seedlings bought from a nursery calls for some skill and patience — you will have to wait for a number of years before you can expect to see flowers (see page 43). Even *Phalaenopsis*, the most popular orchid of all, can be propagated by the amateur grower only by planting up the plantlets which occasionally appear on the spikes. There are several methods for other orchids — these are outlined in this chapter.

DIVIDING PLANTS

The easiest and most popular propagation technique, but two words of caution are necessary. Do not cut up an orchid which has only a few pseudobulbs, and remember that the divided plant may take several years to flower.

With sympodials the rhizome is cut into two or more pieces at repotting time — each piece must carry at least three pseudobulbs. Some people prefer to make these cuts about a month before repotting. Remove old back bulbs and damaged roots. Cut back healthy roots to about 6 in. (15 cm) and plant in pots containing a fine bark mix medium — see page 31. Do not use a pot larger than the original one and stake if necessary. The plants will need more warmth but less light than the original undivided orchid.

With monopodial orchids the rhizome should be divided into pieces which have at least three leafy growths.

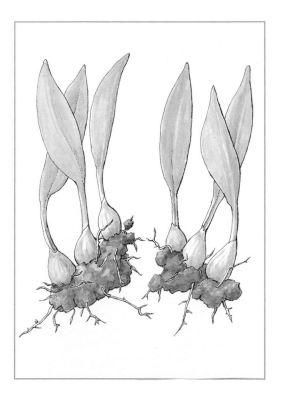

GROWING KEIKIS

Small plantlets are sometimes produced at the bottom or along the stems of monopodials and also on the pseudo-bulbs of sympodials. These are known as keikis — the Hawaiian word for babies, and they can be used for propagation.

Leave the keiki until the roots are about 1 in. (2.5 cm) long — it should now be cut from the mother plant and planted in a small pot filled with a fine bark mix. Spread out the roots and do not plant too deeply. Water carefully and place in a propagator or transparent plastic bag. Repot next season — flowers should appear in 2 or 3 years.

Keikis are a common feature on *Phalaenopsis*, but also occasionally appear on *Epidendrum*, *Dendrobium*, *Aeranthes* and *Vanda*. Useful but not a good sign — they generally indicate that something is wrong with the growing conditions.

TOPPING TALL PLANTS

The stems of monopodial orchids such as *Vanda* continue to grow upwards year after year, and so with vigorous varieties a stage may be reached when the plant is just too tall for its location. In addition some of the lower leaves may fall, giving the plant a distinctly leggy appearance. A few sympodials, such as the reed-stemmed *Epidendrum*, can pose a similar problem.

The answer is to top the plant when it is actively growing. Cut the stem below a node, making sure that there are aerial roots both above and below the point where you plan to remove the upper section. Pot up this cutting in the usual way, inserting the base in the medium and providing a stake for support. It will soon root and continue to grow and flower.

The lower section will also continue to grow, even if it is lank and almost leafless. In time offsets will appear on the stem, and these can be potted up to grow on and eventually flower.

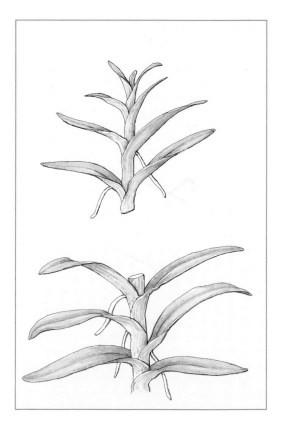

USING BACK BULBS

When repotting you may find that behind the pseudobulbs there are one or more leafless ones — these are the back bulbs. Dark, shrivelled and/or soft ones are of no value and should be thrown away, but hard and plump back bulbs can be used for propagation. Look for a small green or brown bud near the base — this can be induced to develop and produce a new plant.

Remove the back bulb and strip away old papery leaf bases. Cut back the roots, but leave enough growth to anchor the bulb. Plant with other back bulbs in a tray ('community pot') filled with fine bark compost or a sphagnum/coarse sand mix — insert each bulb up to the bud at the base. Mist daily or place in a propagator — keep in a warm spot out of sunlight.

Transplant into individual pots containing a standard orchid medium when both new growth and roots are seen. Repotting at 6-monthly intervals is needed, and the first flowers can be expected in 2-4 years from the time it left the mother plant.

TAKING CUTTINGS

Taking cuttings can be used to propagate only a few orchid genera — the cane-stemmed *Dendrobium* and *Epidendrum* species and hybrids are the ones usually chosen. In spring or summer remove a mature cane — sever it near the base to avoid leaving a long stump behind. Cut this cane into pieces which are at least 2 in. (5 cm) long — each one should have at least two nodes. Dust the cut ends with sulphur to reduce the risk of rotting. Put a layer of sphagnum moss or moss/coarse sand mix in a tray and place the cuttings on the surface — push gently into the medium. Moisten the surface and place in a propagator or plastic bag — keep in light shade in a warm location.

In about 3-4 months there should be some growth above and short roots below. Lift, remove the sides of the cutting and plant each one in a small pot using a fine bark compost.

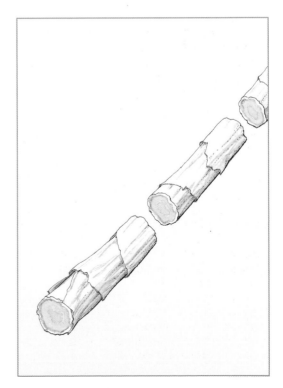

Maxillaria picta
From: Equatorial Plants, Gray Lane
Barnard Castle, Co. Durham, DL12 8PD Phone/Fax 01833 690519

CHAPTER 6

ORCHID GROWING AS A HOBBY

The dividing line between the greenhouse owner who has a large and varied collection of orchids, and the orchid hobbyist who may or may not have a house full of plants is an extremely fuzzy one. Being a hobbyist does not depend on ability or the possession of rarities — there are many fine amateur growers who do not regard themselves as hobbyists, and there are beginners who have adopted orchids as their hobby.

The essential point here is that the orchid hobbyists do more than just grow their favourite plants. There is a range of activities in which they indulge — they may join societies, visit shows, exhibit their handiwork, raise flowering plants from seedlings, go to see orchids growing in the wild, travel to far-off nurseries, and so on. You don't have to take on orchid growing as a hobby to either enjoy their beauty or to build up a collection, but going beyond cultivation enables you to enjoy these fascinating plants to the full.

JOIN A SOCIETY

The first step taken by anyone who decides to adopt orchids as a hobby is to join a society. There are two types:

The **National Societies** look after the interests of amateur growers throughout each country, and they co-ordinate the activities of the Local Societies. Their sphere nearly always covers orchids in general, but there are a number of societies which specialise in a single genus or group. The benefits of membership include a journal at regular intervals plus access to a library, cultural advice and a diary crammed with shows, lectures etc. In addition, trips to nurseries overseas and the chance to see orchids growing in the wild are arranged each year.

The **Local Societies** cover a much smaller area of the country and do not have the same resources as the National Societies, but they do have one distinct advantage. The venues for meetings and shows are closer to home, and this makes it much easier to meet fellow members.

ORCHID SOCIETY OF GREAT BRITAIN
www.orchid-society-gb.com
59 Hainault Road, Romford, Essex RM5 3AA

Founded 1951. *Orchid Journal* published bi-monthly. Meetings are held monthly in London, and two shows are held each year.

ROYAL HORTICULTURAL SOCIETY
www.rhs.org.uk
80 Vincent Square, London SW1P 2PE

Founded 1804 as The Horticultural Society of London. *Orchid Review* published bi-monthly. The RHS is extremely active in orchid matters. Advice on buying and growing.

THE NORTH OF ENGLAND ORCHID SOCIETY
www.orchid.org.uk

Excellent website — well worth a visit. Founded 1897 — the oldest orchid society in the world.

AMERICAN ORCHID SOCIETY
www.aos.org
16700 AOS Lane, Delray Beach, FL 33446-4351

Founded 1921 — the largest orchid society in the world.

READ A JOURNAL

Gardening magazines occasionally have articles on various aspects of orchid culture, but the basic reading matter for the British hobbyist is the *OSGB Journal* and for the American orchid enthusiast there is *Orchids* published by the American Orchid Society. Much of the information is of general interest, and it is therefore worth considering joining both societies. In addition to these regular magazines produced by the orchid societies there is the invaluable RHS *Orchid Review* — the oldest orchid journal in the world. For British growers there is the annual *Golden Guide* produced by the British Orchid Council.

Your orchid reading need not end there. Local societies issue regular newsletters and some U.S societies have their own glossy magazines. There are many informative websites and a host of books for the beginner and specialist.

OSGB JOURNAL

Issued free to members of the Orchid Society of Gt. Britain. A pocket bi-monthly colour journal with society news, articles for beginners as well as specialists, plus book reviews etc.

ORCHIDS

Issued free to members of the American Orchid Society. An award-winning bi-monthly colour journal with informative articles and features plus many photographs and advertisements.

ORCHID REVIEW

Obtained by subscription to the Royal Horticultural Society. A bi-monthly journal started in 1883 with authoritative articles plus details and photographs of award-winning orchids.

GOLDEN GUIDE

Issued free to members of the Orchid Society of Gt. Britain. An annual guide covering society and nursery addresses, events calendar and growing hints plus many advertisements.

SANDER'S LIST

The registration of hybrids began in 1895. The 'Orchid King' Frederick Sander was responsible, and in 1906 the first edition of *Sander's List* of *Orchid Hybrids* was published. Supplements were produced by Sander & Sons of St. Albans until 1921, when the RHS took over the responsibility for the world-wide registration of orchid hybrids and also for *Sander's List*. About 100,000 hybrids are included, and the information is available in both book and CD-ROM format.

BRITISH ORCHID COUNCIL

The British Orchid Council (BOC) represent the interests of amateur and professional growers on the international scene. The membership is made up of many organisations — the Orchid Society of Gt. Britain, scores of local societies, the British Orchid Growers Association, botanic gardens with large collections, the Eric Young Orchid Foundation and the RHS. A Diary of National and European Events is available on the website www.british-orchid-council.info.

VISIT SHOWS & COLLECTIONS

Orchid shows and collections are an important feature of the horticultural world. A **show** is a temporary display of orchids, set out to exhibit their beauty and in many cases to be judged for a prize or an official award. Like orchids, the shows come in a wide variety of shapes and sizes. At one end of the scale there is the local society show in a village hall with plants set out on tables — at the other end of the scale is the lavish Tokyo Dome show which attracts several hundred thousand visitors every year. You can find a show at any season of the year, and they are held in locations throughout the country.

At local shows there will be plants to buy or exchange — at national shows there are lectures to attend and plants and sundries to buy from the trade stands. The Orchid Society of Great Britain holds a monthly table show in London and also two major shows — the Spring Show at Wisley and the Autumn Show at the RHS Halls in London. The British Orchid Growers Association enables its members to show their wares at their Tatton Park Show in June and the two-day Summer Fayre in August. The Royal Horticultural Society hosts a number of lectures and events during the year, culminating in its showpiece – the RHS National Orchid Show in March. Here you can see the latest hybrids from all over the world. In addition you will find trade displays and an OSGB exhibit at the RHS Chelsea Flower Show in May. The show story does not end there. The Newbury International Orchid Show is held in June and some collections hold annual shows — see below. Once every 1-2 years there is the British Orchid Council Congress which moves to a different town on each occasion — every 3 years there is the World Orchid Conference which moves from country to country.

A **collection** is a permanent display of orchids, all of which or only a part of it is open to public view. At Kew there are over 5000 different orchids — some are hybrids but most are naturally-occurring species. In February it shows off several hundred thousand orchids at its month-long Orchid Festival. Another major collection is housed at the Glasgow Botanic Gardens, which stages a Weekend Orchid Fair in April. Other collections can be found at a number of botanic gardens such as Cambridge, Wisley etc and at the Eric Young Foundation in Jersey. Larger nurseries sometimes have open days at which they display their plants and give demonstrations, lectures etc.

For the specialist there are genera collections — the *Paphiopedilum* collection in Christchurch, the *Dendrobium* collection in Glasgow, and so on. The Golden Guide has details. Wherever you are, there is an orchid show or collection not far away.

EXHIBIT YOUR PLANTS

On joining the national or a local society you will be invited to exhibit your plants at one of their table shows — just to be seen there is exciting, and the thought of winning a prize is a thrilling prospect. Your exhibit will be subjected to **Show** (or **Ribbon**) **Judging** — the qualified people involved will decide how your plant or plants compare to its rivals in its class which have been entered by other orchid enthusiasts. If you are skilled (and lucky) enough to be awarded a prize, it may be a trophy plus certificate, a rosette or a gold, silver or bronze award.

All very tempting, of course, but if you are relatively new to orchid growing then you should not rush to take this step. There are two essential steps before putting your favourite pot forward. First of all, go to a few shows to see the standard of entries. Look carefully at the winners — why were they judged superior? Ask one of the old hands — talk to a judge if possible. Next, study the show schedule and rules very carefully — many an exhibit has been disqualified for having the wrong number of plants, being the wrong size etc. The minimum time you must have owned the plant or plants will be set out.

You will have learnt a great deal about exhibiting following your talks with previous winners and/or committee members — it is essential to know what the judges will be looking for. The plants must be well-grown, free from pests and diseases, and with sufficient open flowers to satisfy the judges. Training may be necessary while the plants are still young, but the exhibit should not have an artificially forced appearance. All damaged leaves must be shaped or removed, and extra transit staking may be necessary to prevent damage — these stakes are removed when the display is in position.

QUALITY AWARDS

Judging here differs from the Show Judging described in the other column. **Quality Judging** is the responsibility of the RHS Orchid Committee in Britain and the American Orchid Society in the U.S. Here a plant is judged against international standards by an experienced panel at an accredited orchid show rather than in comparison to other plants on a show bench.

A quality award is made to a plant which is judged to be an advance on others of the type after a careful search of the records has been made. In order of merit the three most important awards are

- **First Class Certificate (FCC)**
- **Award of Merit (AM)**
- **Highly Commended Certificate (HCC)**

A hybrid winning a quality award will have its own cultivar name (see page 4) and the name of the award plus the awarding body can appear after the name of any plant which has been bred from it or its progeny. For example *Vuylstekeara* Cambria 'Plush' FCC/RHS-AOS denotes that it has received a First Class Certificate from both the Royal Horticultural Society and the American Orchid Society.

GROW SEEDLINGS

Buying tiny plants is a challenge for even the experienced and the adventurous — the time lapse between seedling and flowering plant is 4-6 years.

Trying to go even further back by sowing seed at home is not a good idea. The chance of success is slim — nurseries germinate seeds under sterile conditions in a special medium. You can try the natural method if a flower has been pollinated and a pod has begun to form. Leave it to ripen — remove it from the plant when the upper part has started to turn brown. When the pod splits sprinkle some seed on to the compost close to the mother plant – with luck one or two may germinate.

It is better to start with a hobby flask obtained from a nursery — a glass jar containing a number of seedlings in a nutrient jelly medium. These flasks do not need a plant health certificate nor a CITES permit (see page 55) when bought from overseas.

Remove the seedlings by pouring a little lukewarm water into the flask and then swirling out the contents into a dish. Wash away all the jelly medium and then plant the seedlings in a community pot — a wide container filled with a fine bark/perlite mix. Set them about 1 in. (2.5 cm) apart — handle each seedling very gently. Place the community pot in a propagator or transparent plastic bag. Keep the seedlings in a warm and sunless spot.

The seedlings will be ready for potting on in 6-12 months. Remove carefully and plant individually in small pots containing a fine bark/perlite mix. Dropping on and repotting (see page 32) will be necessary at regular intervals until the plant reaches the flowering stage. A lot of work which takes a long time, but you will have the satisfaction of saying to friends who admire your orchid — "I raised it from a baby".

BREEDING A NEW ORCHID

Raising your own hybrid is like buying a national lottery ticket – the first stage is easy but it is almost impossible to come up with a winner.

The first step is to choose the parents. They must belong to the same genus or they must be compatible — if two different genera are chosen consult orchid lists to ensure that they have produced commercially available hybrids. Pollination comes next. Lift the anther cap with a cocktail stick and remove the pollinia — transfer them to the sticky stigma which you will find on the underside of the column on the open flower of the mother plant. If all goes well the flower will quickly fade and the ovary will swell. The green pod will steadily enlarge and should be removed when the upper part changes colour. Place in a dry jar until it splits — this will take between 2 and 12 months from pollination. Shake the seed on to a piece of paper and fold to form an envelope. Write on the details, and now the hard part begins.

The most reliable step is to find a nursery which offers a germination service — the seed is sprouted under sterile conditions and the seedlings are sent to you in a hobby flask. From then on simply follow the advice given in the adjacent column.

The alternative is to sprinkle some seed on the compost surrounding the mother plant, and also around orchids in other pots to increase the chance of success.

The lure to do all this work is the fascination to produce a hybrid which is unique. It may be a beauty, of course, but it may also be less attractive than either parent. Even so, it will be your creation.

Orchid collecting in the 1880s —
this Cattelya skinneri weighing more
than half a ton was cut down and
sent from Costa Rica to the Sander
Nurseries at St. Albans

CHAPTER 7

ORCHID HISTORY

In Ancient Greece Orchis, the son of a satyr and nymph, attempted to rape a priestess of Bacchus. The beasts which accompanied her tore the drunken youth to pieces, and a flower grew from his body parts. Below ground his testicles were transformed into a pair of tubers and the plant was called *Orchis* — and so the orchid story began.

In tropical and subtropical regions there were much more flamboyant members of the family than the smaller ones of the temperate regions, and their beauty attracted the attention of early civilisations around the world. About 2500 years ago Confucius described the charm of *Cymbidium* and some early Chinese painters spent their whole lives painting orchids. In India only the aristocracy were allowed to grow them.

The interest in orchids in Europe centred at first on the medicinal virtues of temperate types rather than on their visual charm. The exotic orchid story began in the 17th century with the flowering of a specimen of *Brassavola nodosa* in Holland. The first recorded exotic orchid to bloom in Britain was in 1731 — a *Bletia purpurea* from Jamaica. The first epiphyte to flower in the U.K was *Encyclia cochleata* in 1763.

Only 15 exotic orchid species were growing at Kew in 1789 — there was some scientific interest in these strange plants, but the gardening public paid little attention to them. All this was due to change in 1821.

The shipment of exotics which William Cattley received from Brazil was wrapped in dried plant material. Green bulbs were present on the dead stalks, and so Cattley potted them up in his stove house. In 1818 the first blooms appeared, big and beautiful with showy rosy lavender petals and sepals. In 1821 the botanist John Lindley named it *Cattleya labiata* to commemorate the grower of the orchid and its flamboyant purple lip.

A stunning orchid rather than an interesting novelty — other eye-catching flowers arrived and both scientific institutions and serious gardeners sat up and took notice. The Horticultural Society of London (later to become the RHS) set up a research programme into their cultivation and orchids began to appear at flower shows.

It was at one of these shows in 1833 that the sixth Duke of Devonshire saw the Butterfly Orchid. He resolved to gather together the largest collection of orchids in the world — see page 103. The seeds of Orchidmania were sown.

These seeds did not germinate quickly, because the gardeners on the large estates and botanical gardens who obtained some of these exciting exotics found them very difficult to grow and almost impossible to propagate. The Duke of Devonshire was lucky to have Joseph Paxton to look after his plants and John Gibson to travel to India and elsewhere to collect specimens. But the early rules for growing were laid down by Dr Lindley. In his address to the Horticultural Society of London he bemoaned the fact that at the society gardens in Chiswick "when we preserved a single specimen of an entire collection we thought we had met with great success". This is not surprising when you look at his rules — a minimum temperature of 80°F (27°C), a constantly saturated atmosphere, heavily shaded windows and no ventilation.

Paxton experimented and sought advice from Gibson and others about the climatic conditions which the orchids had to cope with in the wild. Lindley also talked to hunter-collectors and their joint work evolved into many of the basic rules we follow today. Ventilation was increased in the Great Conservatory at Chatsworth, temperature was lowered, open compost was used, windows were opened and baskets sometimes used as containers. Paxton gets the credit for introducing the concept of Cool, Intermediate and Warm houses to satisfy the orchids' needs.

As the success rate increased throughout the country and as the trickle of new orchids grew into a flood Orchidmania began. From the 1850s no large estate could be without its orchid house and every conservatory of the nouveau riche had to have at least a few examples.

Joseph Paxton originated the idea of Cool, Intermediate and Warm Houses at Chatsworth

Orchidmania was the period when orchids became a status symbol, and the owners of estates were willing to pay ridiculously high prices to acquire a rarity. Specimens of *Vanda*, *Paphiopedilum*, *Phalaenopsis* etc were bought for the price of a house. Orchidmania began in the 1850s and lasted for 50 years, far longer than the Tulipmania which gripped Holland in the 17th century and was as much about buying promissory notes as it was about purchasing bulbs.

Growing orchids in Victorian times was a rich man's pastime — even ordinary varieties were expensive. There were two reasons for this — there was no means of mass production and so plants had to be collected from the wild, and the losses at sea on the homeward journey were almost ruinously high. Disease, rats, insects and neglect sometimes destroyed the entire shipment.

These consignments generally went to nurseries. These organisations were at the heart of the orchid story — Backhouse, Low, Bull, Williams, Loddiges, Veitch etc were all important, but Sander & Sons of St. Albans outdid them all. At their peak there were 100 employees, 60 glasshouses, and they were responsible for the introduction of more than 200 new species.

The orchids received by the nurseries were generally sold by auction — the buyers were botanical gardens and collectors. These collectors were wealthy landowners who wished to amass more and more orchids in their glasshouses.

The greatest of these collectors sent out their own men to trek through tropical regions in order to strip orchids from the trees and ship them back to their employers, and this practice was soon followed by the major nurseries. These men were the hunter-collectors, and their story is one of bravery, dedication .... and greed.

Whole forest areas were denuded — some of the orchids were sent back to the nursery or patron and the rest were destroyed to prevent them from falling into the hands of rival hunter-collectors. As the Director of Kew wrote in 1878 "This is no longer collecting — it is wanton robbery".

During all this feverish activity there was technical progress. In 1856 John Dominy at the Veitch Nursery produced the first hybrid — *Calanthe* Dominyi (*C.triplicata x masuca*). Seven years later he surprised the orchid world with the first intergeneric hybrid — *Laeliocattleya* Exoniensis (*Laelia crispa x Cattleya mossiae*).

Thousands of species and now hybrids, but still no commercially-viable method of propagating them. The first breakthrough came in 1899, when Noel Bernard discovered that a fungus had to grow into the seed to enable germination to occur. Ten years later Hans Burgeff discovered that the role of the fungus was to turn starch into sugar, and these discoveries culminated in Dr. Levis Knudson's epoch-making work in producing a nutrient medium in which orchid seeds were able to germinate. At last there was a technique for propagating orchids.

While all this work was going on Orchidmania had come to an end. By the start of the 20th century most of the hunter-collectors were dead or retired, and the widespread willingness to pay exorbitant sums had ceased to exist. World War I saw further changes. The shortage of fuel and labour saw the closure of many orchid houses — the Great Stove at Chatsworth was blown up by the owner. The interwar years brought another development — nursery-raised hybrids and species took over from the much more expensive wild orchids, and the middle-class gardening enthusiast with a greenhouse became the main outlet for the orchid trade. The end of World War II brought another revolution. In 1966 Professor George Morel showed a flowering orchid which was like no other — he had produced it by growing under laboratory conditions

Charles Darwin established the role which insects play in the pollination of orchids

a minute portion from the growing tip of the mother plant. This was the birth of the meristem technique, and at last exact copies of an orchid could be mass produced — orchids by the million.

Finally, in the 1970s orchids moved into the house plant market. Pots grown in Holland and supplied by florists, garden centres, DIY superstores and department stores were placed on windowsills everywhere. So over a period of nearly 200 years orchids had spread from being just the darlings of the landed gentry to items of room decoration for millions. Now there were orchids for everyone, but the lust for the rare orchid which others have never seen did not quite die with the end of Orchidmania. Orchidelerium has taken its place, and the trade in illegally smuggled rare orchids is immense. A single rare orchid can cost £20,000 or more.

"You can get off alcohol, drugs, women, food and cars, but once you're hooked on orchids you are finished. You never get off orchids. Never."

Orchid Fever (Eric Hansen)

Mealy bug

CHAPTER 8
ORCHID TROUBLES

Orchids are not susceptible to a host of pests and diseases like many other plants. There are some of course, but the lists on pages 51 and 52 are surprisingly short. However, these insect, fungal, bacterial and viral problems can be serious if neglected so speedy action is necessary as curing a seriously sick plant may not be possible. Pesticides are not usually needed — if you do decide to spray make sure the product is suitable for orchids and follow the maker's instructions. Better still — try to pre-vent trouble before it starts. Keep the inside of the greenhouse clean and clear away weeds and rubbish around it.

Most troubles are due to faulty management. Poor main-tenance such as overwatering and lack of ventilation can lead to disease attack, but most of the problems due to doing the wrong thing do not involve pests or disease and these are described below.

"Why won't my orchid flower?"

It's an all-too-familiar story. You buy or are given a Moth Orchid (*Phalaenopsis*) and go on to enjoy the floral display for several weeks. Then the flowers fade, and so you cut down the stalk and wait for another flower spike to appear .... but nothing happens. Your neighbour's orchids come back into flower quite regularly, and so after a year of waiting you decide that growing orchids is not for you.

Try again. The usual cause here is the lack of a large enough gap between the day and night temperatures — there should be a drop of at least 10°F (5°C). In addition your Moth Orchid may be too warm during the day — if it refuses to flower for a year move it to a cooler spot.

Slipper Orchids (*Paphiopedilum*) which refuse to flower may also be suffering from a too-narrow gap between the day and night temperatures. Other factors can be a need for a little less light and a little less water.

A *Cymbidium* which is kept too warm will not flower. Stand it outdoors in summer — see page 80. *Cattleya* needs bright light in winter, and here there is a need for a definite rest period. Failure to provide this will affect and may inhibit flowering.

Each genus has its own special needs and failure to flower is generally due to one or more of these requirements being overlooked. Common faults are:

- Temperatures which are significantly outside the recommended limits.
- Keeping the compost too wet in winter.
- Too little difference between day and night temperatures.
- Failure to provide a satisfactory rest period — see page 25.
- Too little light — new leaves which are darker than the old ones are a tell-tale sign.
- Conditions which cause bud blast — see page 50.

Cultural Problems

DISCOLOURED LEAVES

Reddish and yellow shades usually indicate too much sun in summer — unusually dark green compared to older leaves signifies too little light. Pale coloration may indicate fertilizer shortage.

LEAF WILT & LEAF FALL

Check for pest and disease attack. In otherwise healthy plants the most likely cause is dehydration — see below. Excessively high temperatures can also be the reason for excessive leaf fall.

SHRUNKEN PSEUDOBULBS

Shrunken pseudobulbs and pleated leaves indicate that the plant is suffering from dehydration. Remove the plant from the pot to see if underwatering or overwatering is the culprit. Remove dead roots and repot if overwatering is responsible.

BLACK AREA ON THE LEAVES

Black patches usually indicate sunburn — move the plant to a shadier spot. Black tips are more difficult to diagnose — overwatering is a common cause, but cold draughts or too much light can be the fault. Trim off black tips to restore a natural-looking shape.

BUD BLAST

Bud fall before opening can be caused by a variety of conditions. Too little light is a common cause, and so is overwatering. Dry air is sometimes the reason and so is the presence of ripe fruit next to the plant. Moving the plant when in bud can cause bud blast — wait until the flowers are open before putting the pot in a new location.

Dehydration

It may seem strange that a plant suffering from underwatering or overwatering may show the same set of symptoms. The reason is quite straightforward. If the medium is dry, the roots have nothing to do and so the plant suffers from dehydration. On the other hand if the medium is kept constantly wet the roots rot and so they cannot supply water to the plant — the result once again is dehydration.

Leaf wilt

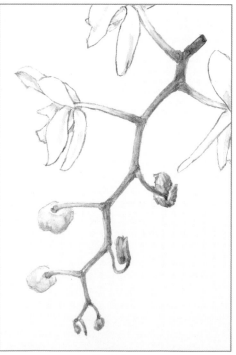

Bud blast

Pests

APHID

Aphids come in from the garden and infest buds and soft new growth — as a result flowers are deformed and pale patches appear on the leaves. Black honeydew mould follows — wash off with water. If the infestation is severe use an organic spray such as derris or insecticidal soap.

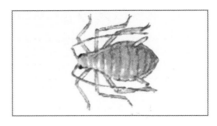

RED SPIDER MITE

Tiny insects which attack soft-leaved orchids — *Cymbidium* is a favourite host. A serious pest when the air is dry and warm — the leaves are mottled with pale patches which turn black. Fine webbing may appear. Spray at weekly intervals with insecticidal soap. False or phalaenopsis spider mite is similar — treat as above.

SLUGS

Buds, flower stalks and root tips can be destroyed by slugs and snails. Clear rubbish away from around the greenhouse and tackle the problem immediately as damage can be severe. Slug baits are available, but the favourite method used by orchid growers is to search for them using a torch at night.

THRIPS

Silver flecking and streaking on flowers and leaves indicate that these minute black or yellow flies have been at work. Buds are often distorted. A pest of prolonged dry weather — usually ignored but if the attack is serious or if you have show plants then an insecticidal soap can be used to control them.

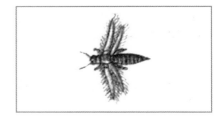

SCALE

You will find these brown or grey discs in the sheaths or under leaves — plants are weakened and leaf fall may occur. The immobile adults are protected from spray by their waxy shells, so wipe off with a cloth soaked with insecticidal soap solution. A paint brush dipped in methylated spirits can be used.

MEALY BUG

These small pests are covered with white, cottony fluff — look for them in leaf axils, pseudobulb sheaths, the underside of foliage etc. The effect can be serious — leaves wilt and growth may be stunted. Tackle in the same way as scale. Mealy bug comes in with the plants — examine *Phalaenopsis* before purchase.

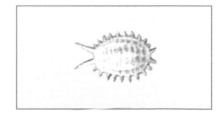

Diseases

BROWN SPOT

This bacterial disease (*Pseudomonas cattleyae*) is specific to orchids. *Phalaenopsis* is its favourite host, but it may attack others. An affected leaf turns yellow and then brown — pseudobulbs can also be the site of infection. The diseased tissue becomes soft, and liquid oozes out of lesions on the surface of the leaves. When brown spot is seen it is necessary to move the plant away from others as the liquid is highly infectious. Cut away all damaged tissue if the disease is limited — otherwise destroy the plant.

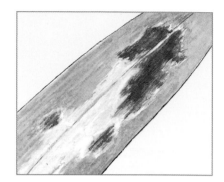

VIRUS

A number of different viruses can attack orchids. Unlike the bacterial and fungal diseases there is no single set of symptoms. Some viruses stunt growth, others produce spots, streaks or mottling on the foliage, or it may be the flowers which are affected. Cymbidium mosaic virus (see illustration) produces pale streaks which later turn black on the leaves. Remember to sterilise all knives and secateurs when repotting, dead-heading etc. Isolate an infected plant, or destroy it if you are sure that a virus is causing the symptoms.

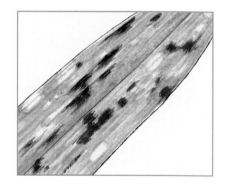

PETAL BLIGHT

This flower disease is caused by the grey mould fungus *Botrytis cinerea*. It is associated with high humidity and inadequate ventilation when the surroundings are cool — it is a greenhouse rather than a living room problem. *Phalaenopsis* and *Cattleya* are the orchids most at risk, and flowers which are past their best are the ones generally affected. Brown or black spots with pinkish edges appear on the sepals and petals. Remove and destroy affected flowers — lower the humidity and increase ventilation.

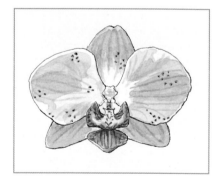

BLACK ROT

A serious fungal disease which like petal blight chooses *Phalaenopsis* and *Cattleya* as its favourite hosts. A soft dark patch with a pale margin appears on the leaf — this rot then spreads, affecting the rhizomes and roots. It appears where the temperature is low, humidity is high and the compost is wet for a long period. Decomposed compost encourages this disease. Take speedy action when you see a diseased leaf. Cut out the patch and a strip of healthy tissue — sterilise the knife after use. Destroy plants where rot has reached the rhizome.

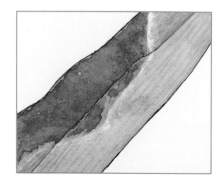

CHAPTER 9
ORCHIDS HOME & AWAY

The word 'orchid' can conjure up a variety of images. For the garden centre shopper it is a Moth or Pansy Orchid for the windowsill – for the bride it is the beautiful white or peach flower in her bouquet. The orchid enthusiast sees a collection of exotic beauties — the naturalist pictures a drift of much more modest flowers in a meadow. For the flower arranger it is a long-lasting bloom which serves as a focal point in her display. Orchids are all of these things, as this chapter shows.

Orchids in the garden

People who live in subtropical areas can enjoy some of the showy epiphytes as permanent residents in their gardens, but for Europeans these plants can only spend a limited amount of time outdoors. Pots of orchids which require Cool conditions, such as *Cymbidium* and *Oncidium*, benefit from a stay in the open air, but they must be brought in before the first frosts.

The garden orchids in Britain are terrestrial monopodials which produce underground tubers or rhizomes which tide them over the winter. The experts are divided on the wisdom of growing these plants in a bed or border. Some believe that it is worth while in mild areas — just enrich the soil with some leaf mould and grit and cover the crowns with a mulch or bell jar in winter. Other experts feel that they should always be treated as pot plants. Use a 2 parts orchid compost/ 1 part grit mix for potting up the tubers in spring — cover the compost surface with grit. Move the pots into an unheated house before the first frosts. Suitable types include *Cypripedium, Spiranthes, Dactylorhiza, Epipactis, Coeloglossum, Pleione* (page 113) and *Bletilla* (page 67). Suppliers are listed in the RIIS Plant Finder.

Dactylorhiza elata

Orchids in the wild

Orchids can be found in every continent apart from Antarctica. They occur in sand dunes as well as mangrove swamps, in valleys as well as high up in the mountains, on trees and stones, in grassland and even underground.

Nearly all our commercial genera are epiphytes which live on trees in subtropical and/or tropical regions. Orchids with pseudobulbs and thick roots have evolved to withstand an annual period of drought — we need to provide a resting period for such plants.

Terrestrial orchids have a wider span of habitats. Most of them are found in grassland or on the floor of woods and forests in temperate regions of the world, but there are many other habitats as shown below. There are some tropical and subtropical terrestrials — the most notable examples being *Paphiopedilum* from Asia and *Phragmipedium* from America. The Slipper Orchids live on the jungle or forest floor and are firm favourites with orchid growers throughout the world.

In Britain there are about 50 orchid species and it is illegal to pick them. All are interesting and some are attractive, but they cannot match the size nor the flamboyant beauty of their tropical cousins. All are terrestrial and deciduous, losing their leaves in autumn and coming to life in spring to produce their flowers later in the season. Many are notoriously unpredictable, appearing as widespread patches one year and then being totally absent in the following season.

Generalisations are impossible. The Heath Spotted Orchid (*Dactylorhiza maculata*) flourishes in peaty moorland but the Bee Orchid (*Ophrys apifera*) needs sandy or chalky soil. Look for the rare Lizard Orchid (*Himantoglossum hircinum*) in sand dunes, but you will find the Bog Orchid (*Hammarbya paludosa*) in wetlands. Spotted Orchids occur widely in large drifts in grassland — the beautiful Lady's Slipper Orchid (*Cypripedium calceolus*) is now only to be found in a single spot in Yorkshire. Our native species are more humble than their tropical relatives, but they are no less fascinating.

CONSERVATION & CITES

Tropical orchids have been under attack for 150 years. The early Victorian hunter-collectors such as Lobb, Gibson, Roezl and Micholitz stripped vast areas of forest and jungle of their beautiful residents — some of these adventurers would destroy all unwanted orchids in the locality to thwart their rivals. As a result orchid populations were reduced and some species became extinct in the wild. The situation is now of course much improved, but this rape of the forest was not just a Victorian phenomenon. In more recent times *Paphiopedilum vietnamense* became extinct only 5 years after its discovery. Fortunately, many threatened species are in cultivation, but the situation is worse for the botanicals — orchids which have been regarded as too plain for commercial collection. Once lost from the wild most are gone forever.

The second threat to orchids comes from forest and jungle clearance which has gathered apace. The removal of trees for timber and for land clearance to create farms, towns, roads etc continues to reduce the number of orchid hosts.

Something had to be done. In 1975 CITES came into being — the Convention on International Trade in Endangered Species of Wild Flora and Fauna, and there are now over 100 countries which are signatories. By its terms trade in some orchids is strictly prohibited — with others a permit for both the exporter and importer is required, and so is a Health Certificate. There are exceptions — trade between countries in the EU is permitted without license and so is the sale of hobby flasks.

Bee Orchid growing on the English Downs

Orchids in the home

The A-Z which makes up the second half of this book contains details of a host of exotic orchids, but the vast majority of the plants grown in homes belong to a mere handful of these genera.

The reason is simple. We buy from supermarkets, garden centres, department stores, DIY superstores or florists. They obtain their supplies from Continental nurseries which offer a small range of orchids — the High St. list:

Cambria
Cymbidium
Dendrobium
Miltoniopsis
Oncidium
Paphiopedilum
Phalaenopsis

The plants offered are generally hybrids and have been selected for their ability to grow under room conditions. The Moth Orchid (*Phalaenopsis*) is by far the most popular choice — it relishes the warmth of a centrally-heated room and can cope with the light limitations of the average room. For an unheated area you should choose an orchid such as *Cymbidium* or *Miltoniopsis* (sold as *Miltonia*) which needs Cool conditions.

Additional genera such as *Zygopetalum* are sold by some larger outlets, but it is unfortunate that with these High St. orchids the label does not state the variety or cultivar. If you want to obtain other orchids in this book and/or wish to have named types, then you will have to buy from an orchid nursery.

Always check the requirements of a genus you have not grown before. Bright light orchids generally need a windowsill and all will require the extra moisture provided by a humidity tray. There are other orchid sites apart from the windowsill. A tea trolley is extremely useful to make moving plants to suit their seasonal needs an easy job. The fish tank terrarium and the orchid case are alternative homes.

It may be that all you want to do is to have an attractive orchid in a pot to enliven an uninteresting part of the room — it is the role of orchids in most of our homes. Just follow the watering rules and the display should last for weeks. On the other hand you may want the orchid to be a permanent occupant — then read the care section carefully. As a single pot, or part of an indoor garden as shown below, orchids make superb house plants.

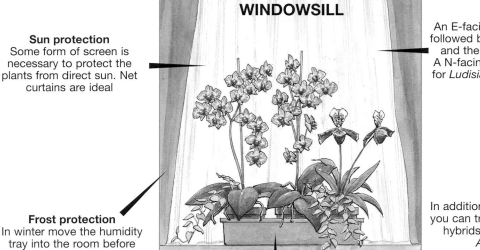

WINDOWSILL

Sun protection
Some form of screen is necessary to protect the plants from direct sun. Net curtains are ideal

Light
An E-facing window is best, followed by a netted S-facing and then a W-facing one. A N-facing one can be used for *Ludisia* and *Phalaenopsis*

Frost protection
In winter move the humidity tray into the room before closing the curtains

Types
In addition to the High St. list you can try popular miniature hybrids of these genera:
Angraecum
Brassavola
Cattleya
Encyclia
Laelia
Ludisia

Humidity
Group plants together — low-growing foliage plants will help. Place the pots in a humidity tray — see page 22

ORCHID CASE

A fully fitted orchid case filled with plants in bloom is a splendid sight in a large room. The problem is where to find a supplier — it is usually a job for the DIY enthusiast. Basically it is a glazed wooden cabinet on legs with a hinged door. There are ventilators above and below, with 3 x 40 watt white 'cool' fluorescent bulbs at the top. A layer of hydroleca pellets is placed in the waterproof base. Water is added — the level should never be allowed to reach the base of the pots. A typical size is 5 ft x 4 ft x 2 ft (1.5 m x 1.2 m x 60 cm).

TERRARIUM

A glass fish tank can be transformed into a terrarium to house an orchid collection. A 2 in. (5 cm) layer of hydroleca (expanded clay pellets) is placed at the base of the tank. The pots are stood on this layer and water is added to cover the bottom half of the hydroleca layer. Do not cover. The advantages of the terrarium are that it provides a moist atmosphere for the plants and it protects them from draughts. The tank can be placed near a window, or fluorescent lights can be fitted above — see page 18 for details.

Orchids in the greenhouse

Moving from the windowsill to the greenhouse opens up a whole new world for orchids. In the living room they had to cope with conditions which were designed for human comfort not theirs — in the greenhouse it is possible to provide the warmth, humidity, light, shade and space required by orchids and not people.

As a result a much wider range of plants can be grown. It has been stressed in the earlier pages and again in the A-Z guide later in this book that the basic requirement is for Cool, Intermediate or Warm conditions, and we have to make a choice. Many choose to keep the house in the Intermediate range — minimum 55°-60°F (13°-16°C), ideal summer maximum 65°-75°F (18°-24°C). This is not quite as limiting as it sounds. Many of the Cool and Warm hybrids can cope with Intermediate conditions, and you can also house Warm-loving types near to the top of the house where it is warmer. Finally, a large greenhouse can be divided with a plastic curtain into Cool and Intermediate or Intermediate and Warm sections.

The pots are usually stood on waist high staging which is slatted or covered with grit. Tiered staging provides extra space and a more impressive show — other alternatives are hanging baskets and slab displays.

You can grow orchids with other plants in the greenhouse, but the keen orchid grower tends to have a house solely for his collection. When buying a greenhouse for this purpose you should look for the features illustrated and described below. Sometimes you will have to compromise. For example, having sides with a brick or wooden base would reduce the fuel bill, but only all-glass houses have floor-level vents as a common feature. So enjoy your greenhouse. Remember that plants don't always follow the rules laid out in the textbook — there is so much to learn from experience!

Water
Having water on hand is a great help. The best approach is to have a water butt inside the house so the water is at room temperature when used

Shading
Protection from the sun's rays in summer is vital. The simplest and cheapest method is greenhouse shading paint applied to the outside. Blinds are the best answer

Insulation
Double glazing is the ideal solution, but even a lining with transparent plastic can cut the fuel bill by 20 per cent. Bubble plastic is an excellent insulating material

Ventilation
Bottom vents are preferred to waist-high ones — see page 24

Door
Sliding doors are preferred to hinged ones — see page 24

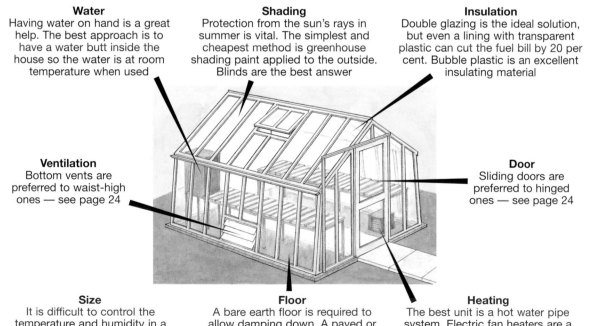

Size
It is difficult to control the temperature and humidity in a small greenhouse. The recommended minimum size is 10 ft x 8 ft (3 m x 2.4 m)

Floor
A bare earth floor is required to allow damping down. A paved or gravel central pathway is necessary

Heating
The best unit is a hot water pipe system. Electric fan heaters are a good alternative — have more than one in the house at ground floor level and with a low fan setting

Orchids in a vase

How times change. A book on flower arranging published in 1989 described orchids as "the caviar of flower arranging — madly expensive, rare, flamboyant ...." and lamented that the Moth Orchid (now our most popular type) was so difficult to find.

Nowadays a range of plants with flowers for cutting or cut flowers in water-filled orchid tubes are widely available in florists, department stores, DIY superstores etc. The great appeal of the orchid to the flower arranger is its beauty, of course, but also its longevity. Lasting for weeks on end, the orchid is indeed the caviar of flower arranging.

BUYING & CUTTING

An orchid bloom bought in a water-filled tube should be left in the container — make sure that it is properly wrapped for its journey home.

When cutting a flower spike from a home-grown orchid you should wait until all the blooms are open and the latest flower has fully expanded. Cut the stalks at an angle and put them immediately into tepid water — let them stand overnight in a cool spot.

ARRANGING THE FLOWERS

Some arrangers believe that orchids should not be mixed with other flowers — they are best displayed in solitary splendour. Others believe that they have a part to play in mixed displays, but all agree that they should be focal flowers which are not swamped by other blooms. Remove foliage which would be in water. Use floral foam or a pin holder to display orchids in tubes.

CARING FOR THE FLOWERS

Stand the arrangement away from direct sunlight and away from the fruit bowl. Every few days remove a thin slice from the bottom of each stalk — be careful not to crush the ends. Top up the water as necessary — with orchids in glass tubes you should change the water frequently.

THE POPULAR TYPES

Latin name	Florist name
Cattleya	Corsage Orchid
Cymbidium	Cymbidium
Dendrobium	Singapore Orchid
Odontoglossum	Odontoglossum
Oncidium	Golden Shower Orchid
Paphiopedilum	Slipper Orchid
Phalaenopsis	Moth Orchid
Renanthera	Fire Orchid
Vanda	Lei Orchid

MICROWAVE DRYING

This technique for preserving large-flowered types takes just a few minutes and the colour retention is excellent. But it is a technique for the adventurous — some arrangers obtain splendid results and others have been disappointed. A layer of silica gel is placed in a microwave-compatible container, the flower with some stem attached is placed on top of the layer and more silica gel is sprinkled over the orchid. A cup of water is placed alongside the container in the microwave and power is switched on for 1-3 minutes. The orchid is removed after 30 minutes standing time. Full instructions for this technique are in The Flower Arranging Expert.

CHAPTER 10
ORCHID DICTIONARY

A

ADVENTITIOUS Growth at a point where it would not be expected — *Aerial roots* are an example.

AERIAL ROOT A root growing above the *medium*.

ALLIANCE A group of closely related *genera* which can interbreed.

ANTHER The part of the *stamen* which carries the *pollinia*.

AXIL The angle between the upper surface of the leaf stalk and the stem that carries it.

B

BACK BULB An old *pseudobulb*.

BARRING Lines or stripes which cross the whole width of a *petal* and/or *sepal*.

BIFOLIATE An orchid with two leaves on each *pseudobulb*.

BOTANICAL An orchid of little or no commercial interest.

BRACT A modified leaf at the base of a flower.

BUD A flower bud is the unopened bloom. A growth bud or *eye* is a condensed shoot.

C

CANE An elongated *pseudobulb*.

CAPSULE The fruit of an orchid, usually called a *pod*.

CLONE An orchid which is genetically identical to others which have been raised from the parent plant.

COLUMN A structure at the centre of the flower which carries the fused sexual organs.

COMPOST A planting *medium* which is partly or wholly organic.

CROSS The offspring arising from cross pollination.

CULTIVAR Short for 'cultivated variety'. It is a variety which originated in cultivation and not in the wild.

D

DECIDUOUS An orchid which loses its leaves at the end of the growing season.

DORMANCY The period when the plant is not actively growing.

DORSAL SEPAL The *sepal* opposite the lip.

DROPPING ON Transplanting an orchid into a larger pot without disturbing the roots.

E

EPIPHYTE An orchid which in the wild grows on trees. The tree is used for support and not as a source of nutrients.

EQUITANT A dwarf orchid with leaves arranged to form a fan.

EXOTIC Strictly any plant which is not native to the country in which it is grown, but popular meaning is a plant which is not hardy and has a showy appearance.

EYE See *bud*.

F

FLOWER HEAD See *inflorescence*.

G

GENUS A closely related group of orchids containing one or more *species*.

GREX A plant derived from a cross between two *species* or *hybrids*.

H

HIRSUTE A plant part which is covered with hair.

HUMIDITY TRAY A water-holding tray in which the pots are held above the water surface.

HYBRID A plant with parents which are genetically distinct. The parent plants may be different *cultivars*, *varieties* or *species*.

HYBRID GROUP See *grex*.

I

INFLORESCENCE The part of the orchid bearing the flowers — the flower head.

INTERGENERIC HYBRID A *hybrid* of two or more *genera*.

K

KEIKI A small offshoot on the stem, *spike* or *pseudobulb* which can be used for propagation.

L

LABELLUM See *lip*.

LIP The modified third *petal* which serves to attract pollinating insects and may act as a landing platform.

LITHOPHYTE An orchid which in the wild grows on rocks.

M

MEDIUM The organic or inorganic material in which container-grown orchids are planted.

MERICLONE An orchid produced by *meristem culture*.

MERISTEM CULTURE A laboratory technique used to produce *clones* of an orchid. Tissue (meristem) is used from the growing point of the plant.

MINICATT A miniature *species* or *hybrid* of Cattleya.

MONOPODIAL An orchid which grows as a single stem, producing leaves and flowers along its length.

MONOTYPIC A *genus* with a single species.

MUTATION A sudden change in the genetic make-up of an orchid, leading to a new feature which can be inherited.

MYCORRHIZA Fungal threads (mycelium) which are found in the roots of adult orchids and must be present in the *medium* to enable seeds to germinate.

N

NATURAL HYBRID A *hybrid* of two different *species* found in the wild.

NODE The point on the stem at which a leaf or growth *bud* arises.

P

PERLITE A planting material ingredient made from pumice stone.

PETALS The inner whorl of flower parts, made up of two upper petals and the *lip*.

POD See *capsule*.

POLLINATION The transfer of pollen to the *stigma*.

POLLINIA Clumps of pollen grains produced by the *anthers*.

PRIMARY HYBRID A *hybrid* of two *species* of the same *genus*.

PSEUDOBULB A thickened or bulb-like section at the base of the stem of a *sympodial* orchid. It is capable of storing water and nutrients.

R

RHIZOME A woody stem which grows on or below the surface and produces roots and shoots along its length.

ROCKWOOL A planting material made from finely-spun volcanic rock.

S

SAPROPHYTE A non-green orchid that obtains its nutrients from dead plant matter.

SEPALS The outer whorl of flower parts, made up of the dorsal sepal at the top and two lateral sepals at the sides.

SEQUENTIAL FLOWERING The opening of flower buds over a period of time rather than all at once.

SLAB A mount for orchids, such as cork or driftwood.

SPECIES A basic member of a *genus* — each one is genetically similar and breeds true.

SPIKE The popular name for any type of flower stem plus flower head. It covers several botanical terms such as spike, raceme, cyme and panicle.

SPUR A tube-like projection at the back of the *lip* of some orchids.

STAMEN The male organ of an orchid.

STIGMA The part of the female organ of the flower which receives the pollen.

SYMPODIAL An orchid with stems which have a limited life. New shoots appear regularly from buds on the *rhizome*.

T

TERETE A pencil-shaped leaf.

TERRESTRIAL An orchid which in the wild grows in soil or surface litter.

TESSELLATION A chequered pattern on leaves.

THROAT The cavity within a tube-like *lip*.

U

UNIFOLIATE An orchid with one leaf on each *pseudobulb*.

V

VARIETY A natural variation of a *species*.

VELAMEN An absorbent white layer on the outside of the root.

Paph Cottesford
'Mont Millais'
AM/RHS

Paph Cottesford
'Mont Millais'
AM/RHS

Paph
Grosnez Castle

CHAPTER 11

ORCHIDS
A – Z

With all commercially-available groups of plants there is a difference between the shop and the nursery ranges on offer. For example, at the garden centre or DIY superstore you will find scores of different roses on offer — old favourites and new varieties all clearly labelled with their cultivar name and growing instructions. A rose nursery will have a larger list, with each rose once again clearly labelled with its full name and other information. And so it is with bulbs, conifers and so on.

The situation is uniquely different with orchids. The shop range is limited to a small number of types which can be depended on to succeed in the living room — *Phalaenopsis*, *Paphiopedilum*, *Cymbidium* etc. No species nor hybrid name is given — in some major stores only the word 'Orchid' appears! For orchids outside this useful but small group and for named types of genera within the group you will have to consult the lists and then buy from an orchid nursery.

As you will see from the following pages there is a large assortment from which to make your choice — with the larger genera only a tiny sample of the various species and hybrids is included. The listed orchids range from ones which are easier to grow than most house plants to others which tax the skill of even an experienced grower. The 'Ease of Cultivation' note should help you to pick a type which will fit in with your experience.

With many genera you will see that both species and hybrids are available. Hybrids are often but not always easier to grow than their parents. The other advantage of a successful hybrid is that it possesses the virtues of the species from which it is derived. The 'best of both worlds' effect is more marked with intergeneric hybrids — a cross between two genera. Here the virtues from the parents may be very different. *Sophrocattleya* is an example — the red colour of the blooms and the dwarf growth of *Sophronitis* is combined with the flamboyant flower form of *Cattleya*.

For each genus in this section there is a list of cultural requirements — the right way to water, the light and temperature to aim for, the resting time to be provided etc. It is important to understand that these instructions are for guidance — they are not cast-iron rules. They represent the opinion of the majority of experts — some authorities may well have different views on specific points. For example, a genus shown here with Intermediate temperature needs may be listed as a Cool house orchid in another book. Furthermore, individual orchids differ in their ability to cope with non-ideal conditions. Some genera are surprisingly tolerant, and even some quite difficult ones managed to survive in the extremely unhealthy conditions which existed in the 19th century stove houses.

The orchid story continues to evolve. In Victorian times *Odontoglossum crispum* was the great favourite — now *Phalaenopsis* hybrids wear the popularity crown. About 3000 new hybrids are added to Sander's List each year — in future editions of this book the A-Z of orchids will contain new hybrids and perhaps new species. In 2002 a spectacular new *Phragmipedium* was discovered. The world of orchids continues to turn.

AERIDES

Typical Flower Form
Small flowers borne
in long pendent clusters

Lilac/pink
and white

Strong
fragrance

Forward-
projecting
curved spur

Pronunciation: air-**EYE**-dees

Common Name(s): —

Abbreviation: Aer.

Growth Type: Monopodial

Natural Habitat: On trees in S.E. Asia — plants may be very large

Ease of Cultivation: Not difficult as a greenhouse plant, but air is too dry indoors

Flowering Season: Depends on type — usually spring or summer

Light: Bright light, but shade from direct summer sun is necessary

Temperature: Intermediate — Warm for some species. See page 16 for details

Watering: Year round — do not allow compost to dry out. Reduce watering in winter. See page 20 for details

Resting Period: Not needed, but reduce water and feeding in winter

Most of the 20 species of *Aerides* are vigorous with upright stems, but a few are compact with a drooping growth habit. The stems bear thick roots between the strap-like foliage, and the flower spikes arise from the spaces between the overlapping leaves.

Moist conditions are essential. There are no pseudobulbs, and that means that the fleshy leaves are the only means of water storage — water regularly and keep the relative humidity at 50 per cent or more.

Repotting can also be a problem — the roots are brittle and some breakage is inevitable. Avoid disturbing the plant unless overcrowding or compost deterioration makes it unavoidable.

A basket is the best container.

AERIDES SPECIES

A. fieldingii

A sweet-smelling species which may be listed as *A. rosea*. The long and narrow flower head may grow to 12 in. (30 cm) or more and is crowded with small blooms which are a mixture of pink and pale purple — the sepals and petals are white-centred. The pendent spike densely covered with flowers is responsible for the common name — the Foxbrush Orchid. Distinguishing features are the flat leaves, and flowers with a short spur and pointed lip.

A. vandranum

A winter-flowering species with 2 in. (5 cm) wide blooms. It is easy to recognise — the flowers are all-white and the petals and sepals are twisted. The spur is large and only a few blooms open at one time.

A. odorata

This vigorous species belongs in an Intermediate greenhouse and will bloom in late summer or autumn. It may reach 5 ft (1.5 m) and so it needs a lot of space, but it is still the most popular species. The purple-flushed white flowers have a spicy aroma.

A. lawrenciae

Another tall-growing species like *A. odorata*, but the flowers are even larger — the white petals and sepals bear magenta patches.

ANGRAECUM

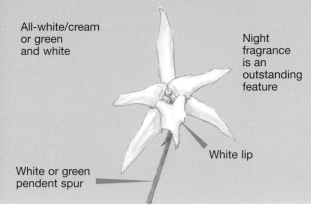

Typical Flower Form
Star-shaped flowers with waxy petals —
several borne on each spike

All-white/cream
or green
and white

Night
fragrance
is an
outstanding
feature

White lip

White or green
pendent spur

Pronunciation: an-**GRAY**-kum

Common Name(s): —

Abbreviation: Angcm.

Growth Type: Monopodial

Natural Habitat: On trees (rarely on the ground) in tropical Africa and Madagascar

Ease of Cultivation: Popular types are easy — small species suitable for windowsill cultivation

Flowering Season: Most species flower during the winter months

Light: Most species require only moderate light — shade is necessary in summer

Temperature: Usual requirement is Intermediate or Warm. See page 16 for details

Watering: Year round. Water when the surface becomes dry — reduce watering in winter. See page 20 for details

Resting Period: Not needed, but reduce water and feeding in winter

The basic form of the flower is simple and the range of colours is limited to white and green, but the size range is enormous. The blooms vary from tiny stars to 8 in. (20 cm) wide giants, and the height of a plant may be a few inches or several feet.

There are over 200 species, but only a few are available commercially. The stems are upright and the leaves are generally long and fleshy with the flower spikes appearing from their bases.

The usual home is a pot, although small specimens are suitable for slab culture. Relative humidity of 50 per cent or more is required, so use one of the techniques described on page 22.

ANGRAECUM SPECIES & HYBRIDS

A. distichum

An unusual species for the windowsill — an 8 in. (20 cm) dwarf with tiny white flowers scattered along the foliage. The leaves are made up of small leaflets arranged in a herringbone pattern — to grow well it needs warmth, high humidity and protection from strong light.

A. sesquipedale

The king of the genus which has a strange story to tell. See page 85.

A. leonis

A short-stemmed species with curved leaves. The 1½ in. (4 cm) wide flower has a large, funnel-shaped lip and a long, curved spur.

A. eburneum superbum

An easy plant which needs plenty of room — it will grow to 3 ft (1 m) or more. The flowers are arranged neatly in a row along the spike — each bloom is pale green apart from the white lip. Provide warm conditions and adequate shade.

A. Veitchii

This hybrid of *A. eburneum* and *A. sesquipedale* is over 100 years old, but it is still going strong. The short-spurred flowers are about 3 in. (7.5 cm) across and the plant will grow to 3 ft (1 m) or more.

ASCOCENDA

Typical Flower Form
Clusters of flat-faced
flowers on upright spikes

Wide range
of colours
available

Small
cupped lip

Pronunciation: as-ko-**SEND**-ah

Common Name(s): —

Abbreviation: Ascda.

Growth Type: Monopodial

Natural Habitat: None — a bigeneric hybrid of *Vanda* and *Ascocentrum*

Ease of Cultivation: Needs winter warmth, bright light and high humidity

Flowering Season: Depends on type — usually spring and summer

Light: Bright light, but shade from direct summer sun is necessary

Temperature: Warm for most types — some are suitable for Intermediate conditions

Watering: Year round — do not allow the compost to dry out. Reduce watering in winter. See page 20 for details

Resting Period: Not needed, but reduce water and feeding in winter

This hybrid genus brings together the bright flower colours and compact growth habit of *Ascocentrum* with the showier bloom size of *Vanda*. The result is an upright plant with strap-like leaves which produce flower spikes from the lower part of the 1-2 ft (30-60 cm) tall stems. The blooms have a more rounded shape than *Vanda*.

Ascocenda is a good choice for a bright windowsill or for growing under glass, provided that you can create a moist atmosphere around the leaves — see page 22 for advice. The roots are thick and a basket is the best type of container. Repotting will cause a check to growth which may be prolonged — do not disturb if it is not essential.

This hybrid bears more flowers on its spikes than its parent *Vanda*. Some bloom twice or even more often during the year.

ASCOCENDA HYBRIDS

A. Yip Sum Wah

The best known *Ascocenda*. It first appeared over 40 years ago, but its abundant blooms and compact growth habit continue to make it a popular subject for the show bench. Brick red is the usual colour, but there are orange, purple, yellow and spotted cultivars. Flowering spikes appear several times during the year.

A. Su Fun Beauty

Well worth looking for. The orange flowers are clustered along the top of the spike and it may flower several times a year. It is one of the easiest to grow.

A. Crownfox

This group of orange, yellow and yellow/white hybrids has some large-flowered cultivars — blooms may be 2-3 in. (5-7.5 cm) wide. Examples of the yellows are **'Moonlight'** (white/yellow with green markings) and **'Yellow Sapphire'** (clear yellow).

A. Meda Arnold

Colours range from red and pink to mauve. It is one of the early hybrids which has *Ascocentrum curvifolium* as a parent, but it is still widely used by breeders.

BLETILLA

Typical Flower Form
Open bell-shaped flowers.
Several borne on each spike

Rosy-purple
or mauve,
rarely
white

Ruffled lip,
darker than
petals

Pronunciation: BLEH-till-ah

Common Name(s): Chinese Ground Orchid

Abbreviation: —

Growth Type: —

Natural Habitat: On the ground in China, Taiwan and Japan

Ease of Cultivation: Easy outdoors in mild areas — keep cool under glass

Flowering Season: Early summer

Light: Outdoors — full sun. Some shade from midday summer sun is beneficial

Temperature: Outdoors — cover crowns in winter. In pots — keep frost-free when dormant. See page 16 for details

Watering: Outdoors — water in dry weather. In pots — keep moist during growing season, reduce water in winter

Resting Period: Winter. Keep pot-grown specimens barely moist — do not feed

An unusual entry in this A-Z section — an orchid which can be grown in the garden in the U.K and most other European countries. There are three basic requirements for successful outdoor cultivation. The site must be in one of the milder parts of the country in full sun or light shade. The soil must be rich in humus and free-draining. Finally, the crowns must be covered with a thick mulch of pine needles, leaf mould or bark chippings in winter.

Plant the pseudobulbs (sold as 'tubers' or 'corms') as soon as they arrive in spring. Set them about 6 in. (15 cm) apart and 1 in. (2.5 cm) deep. In autumn the leaves will die down, and the plant then remains dormant during winter. Clumps can be divided just before growth starts in the spring.

Bletilla can be grown as a pot plant in a cold greenhouse or alpine house where the temperature does not fall below 32°F (0°C). The pots can be stood out or planted out in the garden when the danger of frost has passed. Use a humus-rich potting compost and keep it moist at all times. Feed with a dilute liquid fertilizer every 2-3 weeks during the growing season. Reduce watering when the leaves turn yellow in autumn and keep almost dry until growth starts again in spring.

BLETILLA SPECIES

B. striata

The only one you are likely to see. The 1-2 ft (30-60 cm) stems bear loose clusters of flowers between mid June and mid July. The pleated arching leaves are lance-shaped.

B. striata alba
A rare white variety which is available from a few suppliers — you will have to search to find one.

B. striata albostriata
Another rarity — a pink-striped white *Bletilla* with the same growth habit and flower form as the species.

BRASSAVOLA

Typical Flower Form
Star-shaped flowers — borne
singly or in a small cluster

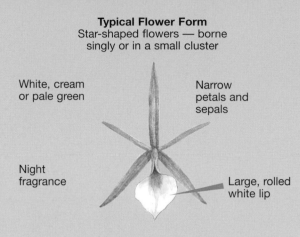

White, cream
or pale green

Narrow
petals and
sepals

Night
fragrance

Large, rolled
white lip

Pronunciation: bra-**SAH**-vo-la

Common Name(s): —

Abbreviation: B.

Growth Type: Sympodial

Natural Habitat: On trees and rocks in tropical
America

Ease of Cultivation: Easy

Flowering Season: Depends on type — usually
summer and autumn

Light: Bright light, but popular species are tolerant
of shadier conditions

Temperature: Intermediate as a general rule —
Cool for some species. See page 16 for details

Watering: Water regularly during growing
season, but allow to dry out slightly between
waterings. See page 20 for details

Resting Period: Necessary for most species,
but not for *B. nodosa*. Keep compost barely
moist for 2-6 weeks after flowering

An excellent choice if you are looking for an easy-to-grow orchid for the window-sill. Most species are compact and unusually tolerant of less than perfect conditions. They grow quickly and come into flower when they are still quite small. High air humidity is not essential for the popular ones, and the night fragrance is a bonus. When looked after properly some of them will bloom several times during the year.

Each pseudobulb bears a single leaf at its tip — these leaves come in various shapes and sizes, and so do the flowers.

Pots are acceptable for housing and so are baskets, but large species such as *B. digbyana* are best grown on slabs. Divide the plant if it becomes necessary, but avoid disturbance if you can.

BRASSAVOLA SPECIES

B. cordata

A compact species with pencil-like pseudo-bulbs and long leaves. The 1½ in. (4 cm) wide flowers are smaller than on the other species. The petals and sepals are pale green.

B. cucullata

Easy to recognise. The petals and sepals are ribbon-like, creamy-white with reddish-brown edging. Both the flowers and the leaves hang downwards.

B. digbyana

B. (Rhyncholaelia) digbyana is the largest and showiest species. The 6 in. (15 cm) wide solitary blooms have ornately-frilled lips. A prolonged resting period is essential.

B. nodosa

The Lady of the Night is by far the most popular species. Tolerant, compact and strongly perfumed — the 2-4 in. (5-10 cm) wide flowers can appear almost all year round.

INTERGENERIC HYBRIDS

B. digbyana has been widely crossed with *Cattleya* and/or *Laelia* to produce large-flowered hybrids with eye-catching lips. See pages 69 and 75 for examples.

Brassolaeliocattleya Rising Sun

BRASSIA

Typical Flower Form
Star-shaped flowers — borne
in two rows along arching spikes

Cream or green
marked with
brown or purple

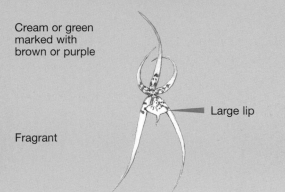

Large lip

Fragrant

Pronunciation: BRASS-ee-ah

Common Name(s): Spider Orchid

Abbreviation: Brs.

Growth Type: Sympodial

Natural Habitat: On trees (rarely on the ground) in tropical and subtropical America

Ease of Cultivation: Easy

Flowering Season: Between late spring and early summer

Light: Bright light, but shade from direct sun is necessary

Temperature: Intermediate or Cool for popular species. Intergeneric hybrids can be kept in a Warm house. See page 16 for details

Watering: Water regularly but allow surface to dry between each watering. Reduce in winter. See page 20 for details

Resting Period: Keep compost almost dry and unfed for about 2 months in winter

The source of the common name is obvious — spider-leg sepals and petals surround the body-like lip. Most types grow about 1 ft (30 cm) high and are a good choice for a large windowsill, but you will have to protect the plant from the direct rays of the sun. An eye-catching orchid to impress your friends — the flower head may reach a foot (30 cm) or more in length and there may be a dozen or more blooms along the spike.

The flattened pseudobulbs bear two or three long leaves and the flower spikes may reach 3 ft (1 m) or more — some support may be necessary. Cut down to a couple of inches (5 cm) when flowering is over. Mist the leaves in summer — do not stand the plants out-doors. Propagate by division.

BRASSIA SPECIES & HYBRIDS

B. caudata
Unlike the other species, this one has yellow flowers which usually appear in autumn. The brown-spotted lip is ruffled. Flower spikes grow to 2 ft (60 cm) or more.

B. maculata
The greenish-yellow petals and sepals have purple markings and the wavy cream lip has brown mottling. Flowers last for 6 weeks.

B. verrucosa

The most popular species and also the easiest to grow. The spreading sepals and petals are cream or pale green, and the white lip bears wart-like dark spots.

B. Rex
This *B. verrucosa* x *B. gireoudiana* cross is the favourite hybrid. The pale green sepals and petals are very narrow and they are prominently marked with brown bands.

INTERGENERIC HYBRIDS

There are several hybrid genera with *Brassia* as a parent — examples include ***Miltassia***, ***Maclellanara*** and ***Brassidium***. Colours are brighter and the flower parts are wider, but the fragrance of *Brassia* is lost.

Miltassia Charles M Fitch
'Amethyst'

BULBOPHYLLUM

Typical Flower Form
No 'typical' flower form —
species and hybrids have all sorts of
shapes, sizes and colours

Frequent feature:
Evil smelling — flies
are the usual
pollinators

Frequent feature:
Hinged lip which
moves freely

Frequent teature:
Small size and
bizarre shape.
Often odd or unusual
rather than bold or
beautiful

Pronunciation: bulb-oh-**FILL**-um

Common Name(s): —

Abbreviation: Bulb.

Growth Type: Sympodial

Natural Habitat: On trees in tropical S.E. Asia, Australia, Africa and America

Ease of Cultivation: Generally rather difficult, but some types are easy

Flowering Season: Depends on type — between spring and autumn

Light: Some shade is needed in summer, but good winter light is necessary

Temperature: Intermediate conditions suit most types. See page 16 for details

Watering: Year round. Water when the surface becomes dry — reduce watering in winter. See page 20 for details

Resting Period: Not needed, but reduce water and feeding in winter

The genus with weird and wonderful shapes — most of the 1000 species have a distinctly non-orchid appearance. The few common features include the presence of a creeping woody rhizome, a pseudobulb which bears one or two fleshy leaves, and flower spikes which arise from the base of the plant.

Leaves vary in length from smaller than a fingernail to longer than an arm, and there are few general rules on how to house them. All should be misted during the summer months and you should not repot unless it is essential.

BULBOPHYLLUM SPECIES & HYBRIDS

B. fletcherianum
This is one of the giant species — the strap-like leathery leaves can grow to 3 ft (1 m) or more, hanging down from the oversized oval pseudobulbs. This is a plant to read about rather than have in the greenhouse — the red flowers have an appalling smell.

B. lobbii
The favourite species — the attractive star-shaped flowers have a pleasant fragrance. It grows about 1 ft (30 cm) high and the 3 in. (7.5 cm) wide blooms are yellow with brown stripes. They are borne singly on top of the flower spike in summer. A Warm house is the preferred environment.

B. purpureorhachis

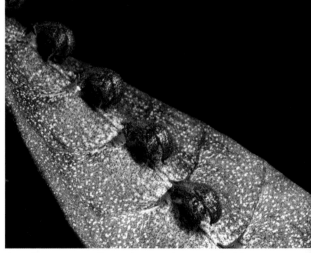

Another unusual species — tiny purple blooms on a speckled, flattened spike.

B. medusae
The flowers grouped at the tip of the spike have 5 in. (12.5 cm) petals and sepals divided into cream-coloured threads.

B. rothschildianum
One of the showiest *Bulbophyllum* species. In winter a cluster of pendent flowers appear — each narrow bloom is about 7 in. (17.5 cm) long.

B. Elizabeth Ann
The pink flowers of this popular hybrid hang downwards — there are knobbly petals above and long, fused sepals below.

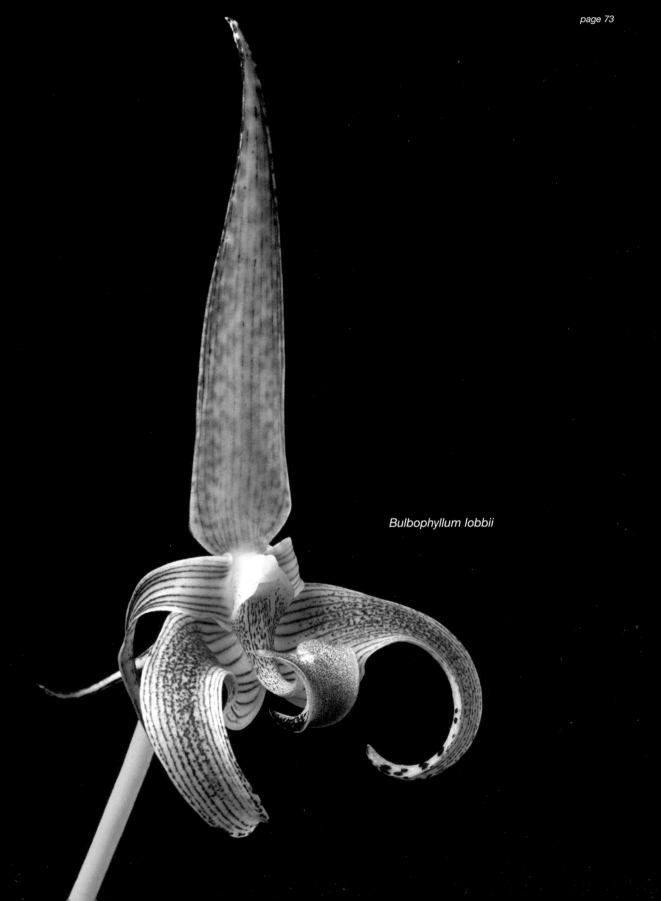

Bulbophyllum lobbii

CATTLEYA

Typical Flower Form
Large flamboyant flowers
with dramatic colouring

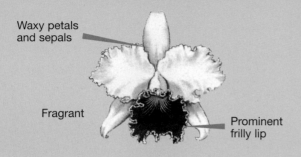

Waxy petals
and sepals

Fragrant

Prominent
frilly lip

Pronunciation: KAT-lee-ah

Common Name(s): Corsage Orchid, Chocolate Box Orchid

Abbreviation: C.

Growth Type: Sympodial

Natural Habitat: On trees and rocks in tropical America

Ease of Cultivation: Popular hybrids: Easy. Species: Easy to difficult — depends on type

Flowering Season: Depends on type

Light: Bright light essential, but shade from strong summer sun

Temperature: Intermediate conditions are ideal for nearly all types

Watering: Water freely, but let the compost become fairly dry between waterings

Resting Period: Allow to rest for at least 6 weeks in winter — give just enough water to prevent pseudobulbs from shrivelling

The showpieces of the orchid world. Here you will find the types with the largest blooms, and the hybrids have some of the most dazzling colour combinations available.

Many of them are large plants, growing up to 2-4 ft (60-120 cm) or more, and so a greenhouse is more satisfactory than the windowsill. But there are the minicatts which reach to only 4-8 in. (10-20 cm).

There are two groups of *Cattleya*. The Unifoliates bear a single leaf on top of the pseudobulb, and there are just a few blooms on the flower spike — usually two. These are the showiest types, with blooms which measure 2-8 in. (5-20 cm) across. There are hybrids which can be even larger. The Bifoliates have two leaves on the pseudobulb and may grow even taller. Flowers are smaller but more numerous — 10-20 per stem.

There are three pet hates — dry air, a poorly-ventilated room, and compost which is not soaked with each watering. Remove the dead blooms, stalks and the papery sheaths after flowering. After a few years repotting will be necessary — carry out this task when new growth starts in the spring. Water sparingly for a few weeks until the plant is established in its new home.

CATTLEYA SPECIES & HYBRIDS

C. Bob Betts

Unifoliate. The most popular white Corsage Orchid of all — popular over the years as a wedding flower. The yellow-throated blooms are 5 in. (12.5 cm) wide. A hybrid of *C.* Bow Bells x *C. mossiae wageneri*.

C. bicolor
Bifoliate. This autumn species has distinctive colouring — the thick sepals and petals are bronzy green and the lip is rosy purple. These 3 in. (7.5 cm) wide fragrant blooms are borne in groups of 3 – 5 on short spikes.

C. bowringiana

Bifoliate. You must give this large and showy plant sufficient space to show off its heads of 5-20 blooms in late autumn. Each pale magenta flower is about 3 in. (7.5 cm) wide — the lip is rosy-purple.

C. labiata
Unifoliate. The first of the commercial showy species. The rosy pink flowers are 6 in. (15 cm) or more across — the tubular lip is reddish purple with a yellow-marked throat. These long-lasting blooms appear in autumn on plants which grow about 2 ft (60 cm) high.

C. maxima
Unifoliate. A 2-3 ft (60-90 cm) high species which bears 5 in. (12.5 cm) wide blooms in autumn. The flower colour is lavender pink — the yellow-throated lip is prominently marked with dark purple veins.

C. skinneri
Bifoliate. The usual flower colour is rosy purple — the 3 in. (7.5 cm) flowers appear in spring in clusters of up to 20 blooms. The variety *alba* is white with a coloured throat.

C. Hawaiian Wedding Song
Unifoliate. A classic-shaped Corsage Orchid with frilly white petals and sepals with a large, tubular yellow-throated lip. Each bloom is about 5 in. (12.5 cm) wide. Other giant yellow-throated white hybrids include **C. Winter's Lace** and **Bow Bells**.

INTERGENERIC HYBRIDS

The most popular choice these days is an intergeneric hybrid. They are generally easier to grow as they are more tolerant of unfavourable conditions than the species, and the blooms last longer.

A number of different genera have been used in these crosses, including *Brassavola*, *Laelia* and *Sophronitis*. New ones appear every year, but their story is a long one — the first *Brassocattleya* was exhibited more than 100 years ago.

Brassolaeliocattleya Pamela Hetherington
A show-bench favourite on both sides of the Atlantic. The 6 in. (15 cm) wide flowers are multicoloured with a strong fragrance. The basic colour is lavender or purple. They appear in spring and are long-lasting.

Potinara Haw Yuan Gold D-J
A *Cattleya* x *Brassavola* x *Laelia* x *Sophronitis* hybrid. Large flowers in vibrant orange — a Grand Champion at the 16th World Orchid Conference.

Laeliocattleya Mari's Song
One of the 'clown' hybrids — flowers with bright coloured splashes on the petals. On this one you will find blooms in a mixture of white, yellow, red and pink.

Laeliocattleya C.G. Roebling
One of the old 'blue-lipped' hybrids with *L. purpurata* as one of the parents. The near-white narrow sepals and broad petals frame the large purple lip, which has the flamboyant shape of its *Cattleya* parent.

ORCHID MISCELLANY

Untouched by human hand

Before independence berok monkeys were trained to collect orchids in Malaysia. These animals had been used for many years to gather coconuts in various countries, but orchid collecting was a specialised activity which called for a long period of training. The monkey clambered up the host tree after being told what to pick by its keeper, and it then brought down the epiphyte as instructed. The champion was Merah, who collected over 300 specimens in the 1930s.

Cattleya skinneri alba

Laeliocattleya Ocarina

COELOGYNE

Pronunciation: see-**LODGE**-in-ee

Common Name(s): —

Abbreviation: Coel.

Growth Type: Sympodial

Natural Habitat: On trees and rocks in tropical Asia

Ease of Cultivation: Most need a green-house — a few are easy house plants

Flowering Season: Depends on type — usually spring

Light: Bright light out of direct sun. Summer shade is essential

Temperature: Cool as a general rule — some species prefer Intermediate or Warm conditions

Watering: Water regularly during growing season. See page 20 for details

Resting Period: Necessary for most species. Keep compost barely moist for 4-6 weeks in winter

Typical Flower Form
Flowers borne singly or in clusters, usually pendulous

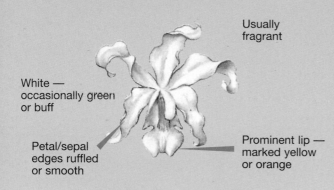

Usually fragrant

White — occasionally green or buff

Petal/sepal edges ruffled or smooth

Prominent lip — marked yellow or orange

About 100 species grow in the wild, ranging in height from a few inches to several feet. On each pseudobulb there is a pair of leaves. A number are grown commercially, and nearly all are more suited to the greenhouse than the windowsill. The usual house plant choice is *C. cristata*, the Rag Orchid. Not difficult, but you must remember to allow it to rest in winter, giving only enough water to stop the pseudobulb from shrivelling. Avoid repotting if it is not essential and grow large specimens in a basket. Keep the atmosphere moist.

The Malaysian and Indonesian species are large plants which require Intermediate to Warm conditions. They do not need a resting period.

COELOGYNE SPECIES & HYBRIDS

C. mooreana
A tall species with erect spikes — on each one 6-10 flowers appear. The 3 in. (7.5 cm) wide flowers have the usual colouring of the genus — white with a yellow-marked lip.

C. ochracea
Compact and easy to grow. Several spikes appear in spring — each one bears a cluster of 1 in. (2.5 cm) blooms. White with yellow and orange patches on the lip.

C. cristata

Pendent sprays of 2-4 in. (5-10 cm) wide flowers appear in early spring. The white flowers have all-white or yellow-marked lips, depending on the variety. Excellent for baskets — it can spread to 2-3 ft (60-90 cm).

C. massangeana
A large Indonesian species with trailing flower stalks. Each 1½ in. (4 cm) wide flower is pale buff with a lip which is prominently marked with white, brown and pale yellow.

C. Memoria William Micholitz
There are not many hybrids from which to choose — this cultivar is one of the best known. The large spring blooms are white with a lip marked with gold. Provide Intermediate conditions.

Coelogyne massangeana

CYMBIDIUM

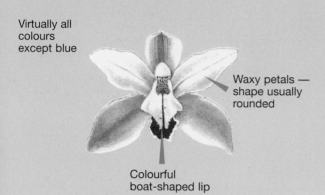

Typical Flower Form
Numerous showy flowers
on upright or pendent spikes

Virtually all colours except blue

Waxy petals — shape usually rounded

Colourful boat-shaped lip

Pronunciation: sim-**BID**-ee-um

Common Name(s): —

Abbreviation: Cym.

Growth Type: Sympodial

Natural Habitat: On trees and on the ground in tropical Asia and Australia

Ease of Cultivation: Popular hybrids: Generally easy.   Species: Mostly difficult

Flowering Season: Depends on type — autumn to early spring is the usual time

Light: Strong light for Standards, but protect from summer sun. Miniatures are less demanding

Temperature: Intermediate or Cool conditions for Miniatures — Cool conditions for Standards

Watering: Year round. Keep compost moist at all times but not waterlogged. Keep drier in winter. See page 20 for details

Resting Period: Not needed, but reduce watering and feeding in winter

Your catalogue may list a number of species which sound attractive and right for you, but these are best left to the enthusiast. Species are generally difficult to grow and the plants are often large and ungainly.

Choose instead one of the many thousands of hybrids which have been bred over the past century or more. They bloom more freely and are more tolerant of temperature fluctuations. There are two basic groups here. The Standards grow up to 5 ft (1.5 m) with 3-5 in. (7.5-12.5 cm) wide flowers. These are plants for the Cool greenhouse — many, but not all, are easy. Miniatures are popular house plants, growing to 1-2 ft (30-60 cm) with 1-3 in. (2.5-7.5 cm) wide flowers. Flower life is outstanding — about 10 weeks for Standards and 8 weeks for Miniatures. There is in addition a small group known as Novelties, with the flower size of Standards and the plant height of Miniatures.

Cymbidiums continue to dominate the orchid cut-flower market and Miniatures are now widely available in garden centres and DIY superstores. There are several golden rules to follow. They do not like high temperatures — stand outdoors in a protected spot during the summer months. Fresh air is vital — ventilate as required in summer.

To ensure that your plant will flower again it is necessary to provide two essentials — there must be at least a 18°F (10°C) difference between day and night temperatures, and the location must be bright with some morning or evening sun. Use thin canes to support the flower spikes and cut down to a couple of inches when blooming is over.

CYMBIDIUM SPECIES & HYBRIDS

C. devonianum

A wide-leaved *Cymbidium* which requires less light but a rather higher night temperature than most other species. The red-lipped 1 in. (2.5 cm) wide flowers are olive green marked with purple. The blooms are borne on pendent spikes — this species is a parent of many cascading Miniature hybrids.

C. eburneum
Unusual — the flowers are borne singly or in pairs on top of the upright spike. The fragrant white blooms have a yellow-marked lip. They are about 3 in. (7.5 cm) wide and appear in winter. Suitable for Cool conditions.

C. tracyanum

The colour of the narrow sepals and petals is difficult to describe — olive green with dull red lines provides a fair picture. The cream lip is spotted with red or brown. These large and fragrant blooms appear in autumn.

C. tigrinum
The late spring flowers on this 8 in. (20 cm) dwarf are unusual. They are borne in groups of three on top of a short spike, each one measuring about 3 in. (7.5 cm) across. The narrow sepals and petals are pale green — the white lip bears red bars.

C. Golden Elf
Miniature hybrid. This compact orchid with 2 in. (5 cm) wide bright yellow flowers has a number of plus points — it is fragrant and it can bloom several times during the year. It is more tolerant of warmth than most, but the blooms only last for about 2 weeks.

C. Summer Pearl
Miniature hybrid. In summer creamy white, pale yellow or pale pink flowers appear on the upright spikes. The lip is heavily spotted and edged with red.

C. Pontiac
Standard hybrid. A popular choice among the red hybrids. Yellow-edged petals and sepals surround the heavily-marked lip on the 4 in. (10 cm) wide spring flowers.

C. Kintyre Gold
Miniature hybrid. A good choice if you want a yellow-flowering *Cymbidium* for a winter display of 2 in. (5 cm) wide blooms. The lip bears red bars and spots.

C. Solana Beach
Standard hybrid. Choose this one if you want really large flowers. The rounded blooms are pink and the wide lip is prominently spotted. **C. Solana Rose** is similar.

C. Nevada
Standard hybrid. Grow this one if size impresses you — 5 ft (1.5 m) tall and with 5 in. (12.5 cm) wide blooms, it is bound to impress the neighbours! The petals and sepals are yellow, the yellow lip is intricately lined and spotted with red.

C. Maureen Grapes
Miniature hybrid. A summer-flowering *Cymbidium* with upright spikes of greenish-yellow flowers. Each fragrant bloom is about 2 in. (5 cm) wide — the white lip is spotted with red.

ORCHID MISCELLANY

Light requirement — nil

The need for bright light for nearly all orchids is stressed many times in this book, but there is an Australian species (**Rhizanthella gardneri**) which lives its life underground in total darkness. The only time it may see daylight is when the autumn flowers occasionally pop up to the surface. Underground insects pollinate the flowers.

It was discovered in 1928 growing in association with the roots of the broom honey myrtle. The pale pink bloom measures ½ in. (1 cm) across.

Cymbidium Summer Pearl

Cymbidium Strathavon

DENDROBIUM

Typical Flower Form
No 'typical' flower form —
species and hybrids have all sorts
of shapes, sizes and colours

All colours
except black
and true blue

Flower size is usually
small to medium —
1-3 in. (2.5-7.5 cm)

Only common feature
is the fusion of the
base of the side sepals
below the column

Pronunciation: den-**DROH**-bee-um

Common Name(s): Bamboo Orchid

Abbreviation: Den.

Growth Type: Sympodial

Natural Habitat: On trees in tropical S.E. Asia, Australia and New Zealand

Ease of Cultivation: Depends on type — some are easy house plants

Flowering Season: Depends on type

Light: Strong light necessary in summer and winter. Shade from hot summer sun

Temperature: Cool as a general rule — Intermediate for some types. See page 16 for details

Watering: Water frequently in summer, moderately in spring and sparingly in winter

Resting Period: Winter rest needed by most types — provide them with good light but only enough water to prevent canes from shrivelling

This massive genus keeps to itself. A few of the 1000+ species have been crossed to produce attractive hybrids but you will not find any intergeneric hybrids in the catalogues. Another feature of *Dendrobium* is the absence of a common flower pattern — *Brassia* has its spider-leg petals and *Aerides* has its spurred lip, but there is no way of readily knowing a flower is a *Dendrobium* if it is not like one you already know.

Plants range from an inch or two to several feet in height, flowers may be tiny up to large, and growth may be evergreen or deciduous. The pseudobulbs may be short and fleshy, but usually they are tall and narrow — these 'canes' may bear leaves. The flowers are borne singly or in groups on spikes from the top of the stems or they may be arranged along the sides. Provide good light, reduce water in winter, provide good ventilation and repot only when it is essential. Keikis sometimes appear — see page 36.

The genus is divided into several sections, each with recognisable features and with shared cultural requirements. Hybrids are often easier to grow than species, and the choice by the non-specialist is usually from one of the two most popular sections — the Dendrobiums and the Phalaenanthes. The star of the Dendrobium ('soft-caned') group is *D. nobile* and its hybrids. The Phalaenanthe ('hard-caned') group is quite different, as illustrated by *D. phalaenopsis*.

DENDROBIUM SPECIES & HYBRIDS

D. phalaenopsis

It is easy to mistake the flower for a Moth Orchid (page 108), but the growth habit is quite different. The thin canes are 1-2 ft (30-60 cm) long and the long spikes of 6-8 blooms are produced at the tips. Intermediate or Warm conditions are necessary all year round. Reduce watering in winter. Colours of varieties and hybrids range from white to purple. May be listed as *D. bigibbum*.

D. nobile

The species grows about 2 ft (60 cm) high and the 3 in. (7.5 cm) blooms are borne in small groups along the semi-deciduous stems. These flowers are white with pink tips — the large lip has a deep red throat. The variety *virginale* is pure white — varieties and hybrids in many colours are available. Cool winter conditions are essential.

D. kingianum

Reputed to be the easiest *Dendrobium* to grow. Sprays of long-lasting 1 in. (2.5 cm) wide flowers appear in late winter — choose from white, pink or mauve with white lip splashed with purple. A cool and dry resting period is essential.

D. lindleyi

A compact species which may be listed as *D. aggregatum*. An evergreen which needs Cool conditions and little water in winter. Pendent clusters of 1 in. (2.5 cm) wide orange flowers appear in spring.

D. chrysotoxum

An orange-lipped yellow species — the 1½ in. (4 cm) wide blooms appear in late winter. Cool conditions and winter rest before flowering are needed.

D. infundibulum

One of the Formosae or Black-hair group — tufts of black hair appear along the stem. The 4 in. (10 cm) wide white flowers have a yellow- or orange-centred lip.

D. victoria-regina

Mauve, but often listed as the Blue Dendrobium. The deciduous canes grow about 1 ft (30 cm) high — the 1½ in. (4 cm) wide flowers do not always open.

D. superbum

You will need space for this giant — the canes grow about 4 ft (1.2 m) high and the purple-centred pink flowers are about 4 in. (10 cm) wide. Needs Intermediate conditions.

D. parishii

The fragrant summer flowers measure about 2 in. (5 cm) across and the floral display lasts for many weeks. The white-centred pink blooms are borne along the deciduous stems. Provide Cool conditions in winter.

D. Thongchai Gold

A house plant hybrid *Dendrobium* in the Phalaenanthe group — it needs Intermediate conditions without a distinct resting period in winter. The long-lasting 2 in. (5 cm) wide flowers have a dark red lip.

D. Andree Millar

An easy-to-grow hybrid which bears drooping flowers. The colouring is unusual — yellowish-green with a large, red-veined lip. The blooms are 2 in. (5 cm) wide.

ORCHID MISCELLANY

Darwin was right

It was Charles Darwin who first clearly demonstrated that orchids were adapted to be visited by specific moths, bats, birds etc which serve to pollinate them. However, he was sent a beautiful, large white orchid (**Angraecum sesquipedale**) from Madagascar which set him a puzzle. It had a 1 ft (30 cm) long spur which contained nectar — but no known moth had a proboscis that long. He predicted that it must exist, but most of his fellow naturalists laughed at the idea. About 40 years later it was indeed discovered — and named Xanthopan morganii praedicta in honour of his prediction.

Dendrobium chrysotoxum

Dendrobium infundibulum

ENCYCLIA

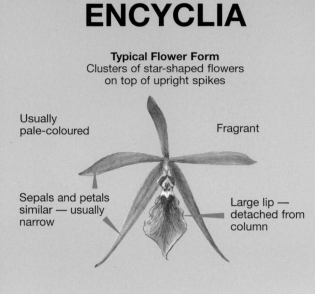

Typical Flower Form
Clusters of star-shaped flowers
on top of upright spikes

Usually
pale-coloured

Fragrant

Sepals and petals
similar — usually
narrow

Large lip —
detached from
column

Pronunciation: en-**SICK**-lee-ah

Common Name(s): —

Abbreviation: Encycl.

Growth Type: Sympodial

Natural Habitat: On trees and rocks in tropical and subtropical America

Ease of Cultivation: Easy

Flowering Season: Depends on type — most species flower in summer

Light: Shade from sun in summer — bright light in winter

Temperature: Cool conditions for most types — Intermediate for some species

Watering: Apply freely during the growing season, but let the compost become fairly dry between waterings

Resting Period: Allow to rest in winter — give just enough water to stop the pseudobulbs from shrivelling

Some of the species of this genus make good house plants — compact, free-flowering and easy to grow. The round, oval or spindle-shaped pseudobulbs are clustered together and from their tops 1-3 leathery leaves and the flower spikes arise. There are a few hybrids, but the choice is generally a species. The plant may have the standard floral pattern illustrated above or the upside-down pattern of the popular cockleshell group (e.g *E. cochleata*), with the lip at the top and the sepals and petals below.

Encyclia is closely related to *Cattleya*. As a rule both will grow quite happily together and there is an inter-generic hybrid — look for *Epicattleya*.

ENCYCLIA SPECIES

E. radiata
A cockleshell *Encyclia* — noted for its strong fragrance and ease of cultivation as a house plant. The 1 in. (2.5 cm) wide cream-coloured flowers have a purple-striped lip — the petals and sepals are shorter and wider than those of *E. cochleata*.

E. adenocaula
The branching spikes on this 1 ft (30 cm) high plant bear pink flowers in summer — the white-throated pointed lip bears red stripes and the column is winged. Grow in a Cool greenhouse.

E. vitellina

Something different. The flat-faced flower is made up of oval, orange-red petals and sepals with a yellow lip. The clusters of 1 in. (2.5 cm) wide blooms appear in autumn.

E. citrina
A yellow species which blooms in summer. Both the leaves and flowers hang down-wards, so slab culture in a Cool or Interme-diate greenhouse is recommended. May be listed as *Cattleya citrina*.

E. cochleata
The Octopus Orchid is an old favourite. It is a typical cockleshell species. The shell-like lip is green with purple stripes, and below the twisted, ribbon-like sepals and petals hang down like legs. May be in flower for many months.

Encyclia cochleata

EPIDENDRUM

Typical Flower Form
Waxy flowers borne singly
or in clusters on upright stems

Green is
often the
dominant
colour

Lip arises from
the top of the
column

Pronunciation: eh-pee-**DEN**-drum

Common Name(s): —

Abbreviation: Epi.

Growth Type: Sympodial

Natural Habitat: On trees (rarely on the ground) in tropical and subtropical America

Ease of Cultivation: Easy

Flowering Season: Depends on type — usually spring or summer

Light: Shade from sun in summer — bright light in winter

Temperature: Intermediate as a general rule — Cool or Warm for some species. See page 16 for details

Watering: Apply freely during the growing season, but let the compost become fairly dry between waterings

Resting Period: Not needed, but reduce water and feeding in winter

In the early days all tree-growing orchids were called *Epidendrum* — as time went by nearly all were transferred to other genera. There are still hundreds of species and some hybrids, and these come in a wide range of plant sizes, flower forms and cultural needs.

There are two basic types. The reed species group has tall, thin stems and needs the bright light and space of a greenhouse or tropical garden. The second group is smaller in both number and plant size — these pseudobulb-bearing species are measured in inches rather than feet. They are similar to *Encyclia* in many ways — the plants are compact and spreading, and the flowers often have narrow petals and sepals with a prominent lip.

EPIDENDRUM SPECIES & HYBRIDS

E. ciliare
Pseudobulb group. The spidery flowers are borne in clusters of about 5 blooms. The petals and sepals are yellowish-green and narrow with a 4-6 in. (10-15 cm) spread — the large white lip is lobed and fringed. Provide Intermediate conditions. *E. nocturnum* (Reed group) has spidery pale yellow or green flowers which are similar, but are strongly night-scented.

E. ilease
Reed group. The drooping stems bear clusters of 2 in. (5 cm) wide blooms over a long period — the pale green sepals and petals are ordinary, but the lip is remarkable. It is broad and heavily bearded.

E. pseudepidendrum

Reed group. The flower has narrow green petals and sepals which are swept back to frame the large red column and orange lip. These 2 in. (5 cm) wide blooms are borne in small clusters in spring and summer. The variety *album* has paler petals and sepals, and the lip is yellow. Provide Intermediate conditions.

E. Plastic Doll
Reed group. A hybrid which is very similar to one of its parents in colour and shape — like *E. pseudepidendrum* it has green sepals and petals and a red column. The lip is yellow.

LAELIA

Typical Flower Form
Flamboyant flowers
with a frilled lip

Wide range
of colours
available

Petals, sepals
and lip similar
to *Cattleya*

Pronunciation: LAY-lee-ah

Common Name(s): Corsage Orchid

Abbreviation: L.

Growth Type: Sympodial

Natural Habitat: On trees and rocks in tropical America

Ease of Cultivation: Most popular species are easy — some types are challenging

Flowering Season: Depends on type

Light: Full light in winter is essential — provide some shade in summer

Temperature: Intermediate conditions are ideal for nearly all types

Watering: Apply freely, but let the compost become fairly dry between waterings. See page 20 for details

Resting Period: Allow to rest in winter until new growth begins. Give just enough water to stop pseudobulbs from shrivelling

This genus is very closely related to *Cattleya* — the only real difference is a technical one concerning the number of clumps of pollen. The flowers of *Laelia* are generally smaller but more brightly coloured — the *Laeliocattleya* hybrids (see pages 75 and 77) are popular, beautiful and numerous.

One or two leaves grow from the top of the pseudobulb, and in the flowering season (usually spring or autumn) long-lasting blooms appear on the upright or pendent spike. Large-flowering types require support.

Plant height ranges from about 6 in. (15 cm) to 3 ft (90 cm) — the compact ones are suitable for windowsill culture.

LAELIA SPECIES

L. cinnabarina
Easy to recognise — clusters of 8-12 bright orange flowers are borne on 1 ft (30 cm) spikes in spring. Each 2-3 in. (5-7.5 cm) wide bloom has a purple-veined frilly lip.

L. anceps
A favourite species which is renowned for its tolerance of temperature extremes. The tall, arching stalks bear 2-4 flowers — these 3-4 in. (7.5-10 cm) wide blooms are available in a range of colours. The standard type is lavender with a lip which has a yellow throat and red stripes.

L. pumila
The one to choose if you want a dwarf. Only 6 in. (15 cm) high, but the autumn blooms are up to 4 in. (10 cm) wide. They are lavender with a yellow and purple lip.

L. purpurata

This showy giant is the Queen of the Laelias — the 5-7 in. (12.5-17.5 cm) wide blooms are borne in clusters of 3-6 on top of 2 ft (60 cm) stalks in spring. The narrow petals and sepals are usually white and the lip is overlaid with purple.

L. tenebrosa
Similar in shape to but smaller than *L. purpurata* — the sepals and petals are copper rather than white and the white lip has a lavender throat.

LUDISIA

Typical Leaf Form
Oval, velvety foliage

Blackish-green surface

Gold or red veins

Pronunciation: loo-**DISS**-ee-ah

Common Name(s): Jewel Orchid

Abbreviation: Lus.

Growth Type: —

Natural Habitat: On the ground from India to Indonesia

Ease of Cultivation: Easy

Flowering Season: Winter or spring

Light: Must be kept away from direct sunlight. A semi-shady spot preserves leaf colour — a north-facing windowsill is suitable

Temperature: Intermediate or Warm conditions are required for active growth. See page 16 for details

Watering: Year round. Water when the surface becomes dry — reduce watering in winter. See page 20 for details

Resting Period: Not needed, but reduce water and feeding in winter

The Jewel Orchids are a small group of terrestrial orchids which are grown for their attractive leaves and not for their flowers. You may find several Jewel Orchids in the textbooks (*Anoectochilus, Macodes* etc) but *Ludisia* is the only one you will see in the catalogues. It is also the easiest one to grow, and you may find it in the house plant section at the garden centre rather than with the orchids. Despite its family, it is just another foliage house plant.

The oval leaves of *Ludisia* are 2-3 in. (5-7.5 cm) long — dark and iridescent above, maroon below. The ½ in. (1 cm) wide white blooms are borne on 10 in. (25 cm) spikes which grow from the stem tips. The fleshy stems creep outwards with upturned ends to form a plant which is about 4-6 in. (10-15 cm) high.

The more difficult Jewel Orchids require the constantly high humidity atmosphere of a terrarium. *Ludisia* is less demanding — it will grow quite happily in ordinary room conditions if you raise the moisture around it with one of the simple techniques described on page 22. A word of warning — do not try to increase the humidity by misting the leaves.

Ludisia can be grown in ordinary house plant compost to which some fine bark may be added. New plants can be easily propagated from stem tip cuttings taken in spring.

LUDISIA SPECIES

L. discolor

The only species — it was known until fairly recently as *Haemaria discolor*. The leaves of some varieties have a reddish tinge. The flowering season lasts for about 2 weeks — the floral display can be attractive on large plants.

LYCASTE

Typical Flower Form
Waxy flowers borne singly
on erect stalks

Usually fragrant

Large sepals around a cup-like arrangement of small petals and lip

Pronunciation: lye-**KASS**-tee

Common Name(s): —

Abbreviation: Lyc.

Growth Type: Sympodial

Natural Habitat: On trees (sometimes on the ground) in tropical and subtropical America

Ease of Cultivation: Usually easy — but some are challenging

Flowering Season: Depends on type — usually spring or summer

Light: Light shade in summer — bright light in winter

Temperature: Cool conditions, but more warmth at night is needed in summer

Watering: Water freely during growing season. See page 20 for details

Resting Period: Allow deciduous types to rest in winter — give just enough water to stop pseudobulbs from shrivelling

Most species and hybrids of *Lycaste* are large plants which need the space of a greenhouse rather than a windowsill. The pair of leaves on the pseudobulb are large, wide and pleated, and the triangular flowers are 3 in. (7.5 cm) wide or more. They are grown in pots as the roots should not be exposed to the air.

Winter is the usual resting period, but a few species continue to grow at this time — the rule is to reduce watering when growth ceases. Moist air around the leaves is needed for all types.

Apart from the species there are a number of attractive hybrids. The intergeneric hybrid *Angulocaste* (*Anguloa* x *Lycaste*) is a good choice.

LYCASTE SPECIES & HYBRIDS

L. aromatica
A compact species which is suitable for the windowsill. Numerous flower spikes are produced, and the 3 in. (7.5 cm) wide yellow flowers have a cinnamon-like fragrance.

L. cruenta
Rather similar to *L. aromatica* — dwarf, yellow-flowered and cinnamon-scented. The blooms, however, are larger and the sepals are greenish yellow. The golden yellow lip has a red-spotted throat.

L. virginalis
There is no clear line between this species and *L. skinneri*, and so they are often lumped together. This is the one to choose for the largest flowers — 4-6 in. (10-15 cm) wide blooms in white or pink in winter.

L. deppei

An early spring species with 4 in. (10 cm) wide blooms which has a combination of colours. The sepals are green with dull red spots and blotches, the petals are white and the yellow lip has red spots.

L. Andy Easton
This red hybrid is an example of the colourful crosses which have been bred using a deep pink variety of *L. virginalis* as a parent.

MASDEVALLIA

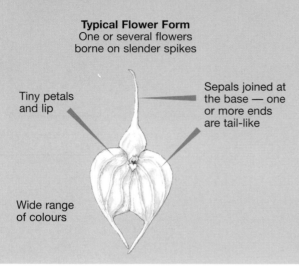

Typical Flower Form
One or several flowers
borne on slender spikes

Tiny petals
and lip

Sepals joined at
the base — one
or more ends
are tail-like

Wide range
of colours

Pronunciation: maz-de-**VAL**-ee-ah

Common Name(s): Kite Orchid

Abbreviation: Masd.

Growth Type: Sympodial

Natural Habitat: On trees and rocks in tropical and subtropical America

Ease of Cultivation: Some hybrids are easy, but species can be challenging

Flowering Season: Depends on type — usually summer

Light: Some shade is needed all year round

Temperature: Cool conditions — a hot stuffy room can be a problem in summer. See page 16 for details

Watering: Year round. Compost should be moist, but never let it become waterlogged. Keep drier in winter. See page 20 for details

Resting Period: Not needed, but reduce water and feeding in winter

Masdevallias have a wide variety of shapes, but it is nearly always easy to recognise them from the distinctive shape of the sepals. One or more have narrow tails, giving this orchid its common name. The rhizomes produce short stems and from the top of each one grows a single fleshy leaf. There are no pseudobulbs.

A number of very attractive hybrids are available, and these are generally easier to grow than the species. All of them have several special needs. High summer temperatures over 80°F (27°C) pose a problem and bright light is unacceptable. Watering should not be a problem as there is no resting period to think about, but you must be careful not to keep the compost soggy as the roots readily rot. Roots should not be exposed to the air, so *Masdevallia* is not suitable for basket nor slab display.

MASDEVALLIA SPECIES & HYBRIDS

M. tovanensis

Several white flowers appear on each short stalk in winter. The upper sepal is a long narrow tube — the broad side ones have short tails which often cross each other. Do not cut down the stalks after flowering — you can expect it to bloom again next year.

M. coccinea

There is a single rounded flower on a tall stalk — the 2 in. (5 cm) wide bloom has a narrow upper sepal and two semi-circular side ones. Red is the usual colour, but white, yellow and pink varieties are available.

M. veitchiana

A colourful species which has been widely used to produce a number of eye-catching hybrids. The large, early summer flowers are bright orange — a novel feature is the covering of short purple hairs.

M. Copper Angel

This dwarf hybrid has *M. veitchiana* as one of its parents. The orange blooms have an even triangular shape — each sepal ends in a long thin tail.

MILTONIA

Typical Flower Form
One or several flowers on
arching or upright spikes

Strap-like
petals and
sepals

Large flat lip

Pronunciation: mil-**TONE**-ee-ah

Common Name(s): —

Abbreviation: Milt.

Growth Type: Sympodial

Natural Habitat: On trees in Brazil and Venezuela

Ease of Cultivation: Rather demanding —
easiest ones are listed here

Flowering Season: Depends on type — usually
summer or autumn

Light: Shade from direct sunlight is necessary

Temperature: Intermediate conditions — needs
warmer conditions than *Miltoniopsis*. See page
16 for details

Watering: Year round. Keep compost moist at all
times but not waterlogged. Reduce watering in
winter. See page 20 for details

Resting Period: Not needed, but reduce water
and feeding in winter

The Pansy Orchids at garden centres are sold as *Miltonia*, but they are really hybrids of the genus described on pages 96-97. Unlike the *Miltoniopsis* orchids the flowers of the species listed here do not have a pansy-like appearance, and there are two leaves rather than a single one arising from each pseudobulb. They grow 1-1½ ft (30-45 cm) high and the flowers measure 1-3 in. (2.5-7.5 cm) across.

Miltonia species are sometimes recommended as windowsill plants for the beginner, but they are better left to the experienced grower with a green-house. The problem is that they do not like fluctuating conditions — they need constantly moist air, and compost which is kept moist but never waterlogged. The night/day temperature fluctuation should ideally be less than 10°F (5°C). *Miltonia* is suitable for both pot and basket culture.

MILTONIA SPECIES & HYBRIDS

M. flavescens
The sepals and petals are pale yellow rather than white, pink or purple, and the red-spotted white lip is small. The 3 in. (7.5 cm) wide flowers are clustered on the top of the 1 ft (30 cm) high spike.

M. regnellii
The petals and sepals are white with a pink flush — the pink lip is streaked with pale purple lines. The 3 in. (7.5 cm) wide fragrant blooms appear in late summer.

M. spectabilis

The most popular species — flowers are borne singly on 10 in. (25 cm) spikes. The usual colour is white tinged with pink, but white and purple varieties are available. The lip has dark pink blotches and lines.

M. Anne Warne
A single purple flower is borne on the spike. The lip is large and veined.

MILTONIOPSIS

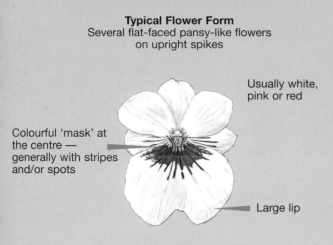

Typical Flower Form
Several flat-faced pansy-like flowers
on upright spikes

Usually white,
pink or red

Colourful 'mask' at
the centre —
generally with stripes
and/or spots

Large lip

Pronunciation: mil-tone-ee-**OP**-sis

Common Name(s): Pansy Orchid

Abbreviation: Mps.

Growth Type: Sympodial

Natural Habitat: On trees in Colombia, Peru, Costa Rica and Ecuador

Ease of Cultivation: Popular hybrids are reasonably easy — species are demanding

Flowering Season: Depends on type — usually spring or autumn

Light: Shade from direct sunlight is necessary

Temperature: Cool conditions — try to avoid sudden and wide changes. See page 16 for details

Watering: Year round. Keep compost moist at all times but not waterlogged. Reduce watering in winter. See page 20 for details

Resting Period: Not needed, but reduce water and feeding in winter

In garden centres and DIY superstores you will find these attractive orchids labelled as *Miltonia*. They are actually *Miltoniopsis* hybrids — thousands of these crosses have been produced and many of them are suitable for the living room. Species, however, are rare and belong in the specialist collection.

The plants are compact but the blooms are large. The feature to look for is the distinctive 'mask' — a central splash of colour in a wide variety of shapes. The blooms are long-lasting on the spike, but die rapidly when cut for flower arranging. The 'waterfall' types have radiating lines of spots.

The care rules for *Miltonia* apply, but the hybrids listed here benefit from cooler conditions, and tend to be more tolerant of fluctuations. Humid air is needed, but don't mist the leaves. Aim to keep them in the 50°-80°F (10°-27°C) range.

MILTONIOPSIS SPECIES & HYBRIDS

M. St. Helier
A good example of the Jersey hybrids which play such an important part in the *Miltoniopsis* story. The basic colour is pink or red — the mask is dark red with a broad white margin and veining below.

M. vexillaria

Included here because it is one of the basic parents of most hybrids. The flower is large but the white or rose petals are small. The yellow-centred rose lip bears fine pink veins. The flowering period is early summer.

M. Dainty Miss
Compact and free-flowering. The blooms are white flushed with pink — the 'waterfall' pattern on the mask is red with a yellow base.

M. Hajime Ono
Spectacular. Rich red with a narrow white outline — the eye-catching lip has a mask which is a dark red 'waterfall' clearly outlined in white.

Miltoniopsis Celle
'Waterfall'

ODONTOGLOSSUM

Typical Flower Form
Numerous showy flowers
on arching stems

Hybrids in many colours — often blotched

Species sometimes spidery — hybrids usually rounded

Petals and sepals ruffled — lip often crested

Pronunciation: oh-don-toh-**GLOSS**-um

Common Name(s): —

Abbreviation: Odm.

Growth Type: Sympodial

Natural Habitat: On trees and rocks in tropical and subtropical America

Ease of Cultivation: Some hybrids are easy. Species are generally difficult

Flowering Season: Depends on type

Light: Summer shade is necessary — a north- or west-facing window is suitable for house plant hybrids

Temperature: Cool conditions are ideal for nearly all types

Watering: Year round. Keep compost moist but not waterlogged at all times. Keep drier in winter. See page 20 for details

Resting Period: Not needed, but reduce water and feeding in winter

Among the *Odontoglossum* species and hybrids you will find some of the most beautiful of all orchids. The Victorians were fascinated by the species, but not many are now offered. These are generally not easy and are best left to the specialist grower. Choose instead one of the hybrids, which are easier to grow. These hybrids nearly always involve other genera, and among these intergeneric hybrids you will find the most beautiful types.

The usual form at flowering time is a single spike about 1½ ft (45 cm) high with a dozen or more flowers at the top. Flowering does not follow a regular 12-month cycle, and in a large collection it is possible to have plants in flower almost all year round. The flowers are in a wide variety of shapes and sizes, and are long-lasting. At the base of the flower spike are the pseudobulbs — egg-shaped with small leaves below and a pair of larger leaves at the top.

The major problem is the dislike of warm conditions. *Odontoglossum* species and some of their hybrids begin to suffer when the room temperature reaches 80°F (27°C) — fortunately the popular intergeneric hybrids (see page 99) are more tolerant. Another pet hate is dry air — some method of raising the humidity of the surrounding air is necessary. Finally, remember that the plants described here do not need quite as much light as the average orchid.

ODONTOGLOSSUM SPECIES & HYBRIDS

O. crispum

This 4 in. (10 cm) wide flower is regarded by many as the most beautiful of the species. The basic colour is white, but over the years there have been innumerable varieties — pink or purple flushed, red or purple blotched, and edges which are smooth or deeply toothed. The lip is marked with yellow.

O. grande

The label may say *Odontoglossum* but the botanical name for the Tiger Orchid is *Rossioglossum grande*. The source of the common name is obvious. The yellow sepals have brown stripes, the petals are yellow and brown, and the white lip is spotted. The spidery blooms are 6 in. (15 cm) wide.

O. pulchellum

The 1 ft (30 cm) spike bears sprays of waxy 1 in. (2.5 cm) wide flowers in winter. These white blooms have a yellow centre and a sweet fragrance — hence the common name of Lily-of-the-Valley Orchid.

O. Geyser Gold

This hybrid is included as it is the most popular member of a small group which are reliable house plants. It is less demanding than the popular types, and the 2 in. (5 cm) wide blooms are unusual. The base colour of the bloom is pale yellow and white, and is overlaid with dark yellow blotches.

INTERGENERIC HYBRIDS

For more than 100 years plant breeders have crossed *Odontoglossum* with genera which belong to its close relatives which make up the Odontoglossum Alliance. As a result there are plants with a much wider range of shapes and sizes, a multitude of different colours and complex patterns, and a wider tolerance of less-than-perfect heating and watering. Examples include *Adaglossum, Beallara, Colmanara, Odontioda, Odontobrassia, Odontocidium, Odontonia, Sanderana, Vuylstekeara* and *Wilsonara*. Some of the more popular ones are described below — *Vuylstekeara* is described separately on page 118.

Odontocidium Purbeck Gold

(*Odontoglossum* x *Oncidium*) Odontoglossum-like 3 in. (7.5 cm) wide flowers with the flared lip and colours of *Oncidium*. This typical example has yellow petals and sepals with brown markings.

Beallara Tahoma Glacier

(*Odontoglossum* x *Brassia* x *Cochlioda* x *Miltonia*) A large-flowered hybrid which will thrive in Cool or Intermediate conditions. Most have white or pale-coloured blooms with purple markings — this one is green-tinged white with purple spots and lines. The sepals and petals are generally narrow.

Odontioda Margaret Holm

(*Odontoglossum* x *Cochlioda*) The usual flower form is the shape of *Odontoglossum* and the colours of *Cochlioda*. This was the first of the intergeneric hybrids and remains the most popular. The base colour is generally white or pink with an intricate patterning of pink or red. This one is white with dark red lines and spots.

Colmanara Wildcat

(*Odontoglossum* x *Oncidium* x *Miltonia*) The waxy flowers are yellow with red markings — they will grow in an Intermediate or even a Warm house. This vigorous example has white or yellow flowers with an intricate pattern of red spots and splashes.

Odontonia Boussole 'Blanche'

(*Odontoglossum* x *Miltonia*) This cultivar is the most popular *Odontonia* and is a good example of this genus. The 3 in. (7.5 cm) blooms are white or pale pink with two large red patches. The colourful lip is flared.

ORCHID MISCELLANY

The orchid in the kitchen

*The Spanish Conquistadores found that the Aztecs used an extract of an orchid to flavour their cocoa drink. They named it **Vanilla** ('little pod'), and over the years it has been sold as an aphrodisiac and medicine as well as a flavouring agent. Several species are grown commercially for the vanillin extracted from the seed capsules, but the bottle on your kitchen shelf is likely to contain a synthetic substitute.*

Odontioda
Lyoth Alpha

Odontoglossum Royal Ballerina

ONCIDIUM

Typical Flower Form
Masses of fluttering flowers on top of tall, arching stems

Yellow, with brown markings. Other colours — white, pink, purple, green

Body-like upper part of flower — hence the common name

Flared skirt-like lip

Pronunciation: on-SID-ee-um

Common Name(s): Dancing Lady

Abbreviation: Onc.

Growth Type: Sympodial

Natural Habitat: On trees (rarely on the ground) in tropical and subtropical America

Ease of Cultivation: Popular hybrids: Easy. Species: Easy to difficult — depends on type

Flowering Season: Depends on type — usually autumn

Light: Good light, but not direct sunlight. Thick-leaved types need strong light

Temperature: Cool or Intermediate. Warm for some species. See page 16 for details

Watering: Hybrids: Year round — reduce in winter. Species: Keep dry when growth stops. See page 20 for details

Resting Period: Hybrids: Not needed. Species: Allow to rest in winter

Oncidium species have been around for a long time. There were specimens at Kew at the end of the 18th century, and it was this orchid which led to the craze known as Orchidmania — see page 103.

It is a large and highly varied genus, with about 400 species and even more hybrids. They range from the miniature equitants with their fans of iris-like leaves to the giant species with thick 'mule-ear' leaves and yard-long sprays of flowers.

The hybrids listed in this section are generally regarded as suitable for the beginner's windowsill. Clay and plastic pots make suitable containers, and for many of them with long and pendent sprays of flowers you can create a basket or slab display. Don't be afraid to cut back the flowering stems if they grow too long — branching out will often occur with another crop of flowers. Standing the pot outdoors in summer is recommended.

The species offer more of a challenge — they belong in the greenhouse and you will have to keep the temperature under control in summer. Both good ventilation and regular damping down are necessary. Reliable cool house ones include *O. crispum* and *O. flexuosum* — the equitants need warm and moist air throughout the year.

When repotting is necessary, you should wait until you can see new growth beginning to appear.

ONCIDIUM SPECIES

O. crispum
The large flowers with wavy-edged petals are a departure from the usual yellow and brown. With its reddish-brown colour and yellow-throated lip it is one of the showiest species. The branched spikes reach about 12 in. (30 cm).

O. sphaceletum

A tall and easy species which belongs in the cool conservatory or greenhouse rather than in the living room. The flowers are yellow with brown markings, and the branched spikes grow to 3 ft (1 m) or more. Where possible, plant in a basket or on a slab.

O. flexuosum

The small flowers are clustered at the ends of the 2 ft (60 cm) spikes. They appear in autumn and bear the typical colour of the genus — yellow with brown markings.

O. tigrinum

This species needs space for its tall and arching spikes which may reach 3 ft (1 m) or more — a Cool greenhouse is the ideal home. The flowers are 2 in. (5 cm) wide and the colour is yellow with brown stripes.

O. ornithorhynchum

A compact species with arching spikes above the 8 in. (20 cm) high foliage. The lilac or pink 1 in. (2.5 cm) wide flowers are yellow-crested at the centre, and there is a strong vanilla-like fragrance.

INTERGENERIC HYBRIDS

Burrageara Glowing Embers

A number of excellent hybrid genera have been produced by using *Oncidium* as one of the parents. Pictured above is a cross between *Oncidium*, *Odontoglossum*, *Cochlioda* and *Miltonia*. There are numerous others, including **Colmanara**, **Wilsonara**, **Vuylstekeara** (page 118), **Odontocidium** and **Aliceara**. The object of the hybridist has been to combine interesting flower shapes with an improved tolerance of a wide range of conditions.

ONCIDIUM HYBRIDS

O. Sharry Baby

A favourite on both sides of the Atlantic — the white-lipped cherry red flowers are 1 in. (2.5 cm) wide and easily recognised by their pronounced chocolate-bar fragrance. Vigorous and free-flowering, the branched spikes reach about 2 ft (60 cm) and they appear at various times of the year. This hybrid prefers cool conditions.

O. Tsiku Marguerite

An easy one for the windowsill or cool greenhouse. It is a compact hybrid reaching about 6 in. (15 cm) — the branched spikes bear masses of 1 in. (2.5 cm) wide creamy flowers. Another beginner *Oncidium* is O. Star Wars.

O. Twinkle

Look no further if you want a dwarf *Oncidium* with a strong fragrance. The drooping spikes appear in succession and grow to about 8 in. (20 cm). The 1 in. (2.5 cm) wide flowers appear in spring and autumn, and white, cream, pink and red cultivars are available.

O. Gower Ramsey

Masses of 1/2 in. (1 cm) blooms are borne on tall spikes — you can expect it to flower twice a year. Small-flowered hybrids such as this one are the easiest to grow, and are remarkably tolerant of conditions which are less than ideal.

ORCHID MISCELLANY

The orchid that began it all

In 1826 the Governor of Trinidad brought plants of **Oncidium papilio** to England, and in 1833 specimens in bloom were exhibited at the Horticultural Society of London. The sixth Duke of Devonshire attended the show and was utterly captivated by the butterfly-like blooms.

He became an avid collector, and his enthusiasm for orchids slowly spread to wealthy landowners around the country. Collectors began to comb the tropics for new species, and this widespread interest steadily increased until it became the Orchidmania starting in the 1850s.

The butterfly orchid has changed its name to **Psychopsis papilio**, but its charm remains.

PAPHIOPEDILUM

Pronunciation: paff-ee-oh-**PED**-ee-lum

Common Name(s): Slipper Orchid

Abbreviation: Paph.

Growth Type: Sympodial

Natural Habitat: On the ground (occasionally on rocks and trees) in tropical and subtropical Asia

Ease of Cultivation: Popular hybrids are easy — some species are challenging

Flowering Season: Depends on type — a collection can be in bloom all year round

Light: Less light required than for most other orchids — shade from direct sunlight

Temperature: Cool, Intermediate or Warm conditions, depending on type

Watering: Year round. Compost should be kept moist, but never let it become waterlogged

Resting Period: Not needed, but reduce water and feeding in winter

Typical Flower Form
Flowers borne singly or in small clusters on top of upright hairy spikes

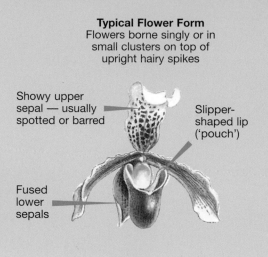

Showy upper sepal — usually spotted or barred

Slipper-shaped lip ('pouch')

Fused lower sepals

A distinct group of orchids which are suitable for room cultivation and are available in garden centres, DIY superstores, supermarkets and department stores everywhere. The common name is derived from the shape of the flower.

This orchid has been a great favourite with both beginners and specialist growers for many years, and it has several unusual features. The showy flowers bear a distinctive pouch which captures insects, and there are no pseudobulbs. Several leaves are joined at the base to form a fan, and they are often attractive enough to provide a foliage house plant display all year round. Another unusual feature is the inability to propagate these plants by meristem culture — see page 47. This means that all specimens are produced from seed or by division.

Mottled-leaved hybrids are easy to grow on shaded windowsills or under fluorescent lights. The usual flower width is 3-5 in. (7.5-12.5 cm) and they last for up to 3 months. Among the thousands of hybrids there are waxy flowers in a wide range of shapes and vibrant colours.

The traditional rule is that the plain green-leaved types should be kept under Cool conditions, and the mottled ones should be given more shade and Intermediate conditions. Hybrids, however, are the usual types which are on offer, and all of them will flourish in Intermediate or even Warm surroundings.

You will need to increase the air humidity. A humidity tray is the easiest way. Misting is not a good idea as moisture at the base of the leaves can cause rotting — wiping the leaves with a damp cloth is better. Constantly soggy soil is the main cause of death, and red spider mite is the main pest. Repot into a plastic pot every 1-2 years and never stand it outdoors. Very simply, an orchid for everyone.

PAPHIOPEDILUM SPECIES & HYBRIDS

P. bellatum
Mottled-leaved type. Quite distinctive for two reasons — the 3 in. (7.5 cm) wide bloom rests on top of the broad leaves, and the petals are larger than the upper sepal. The flower colour is white or pale yellow with tiny purple spots.

P. delenatii
Mottled-leaved type. The broad leaves are beautifully marbled and the fragrant flowers appear in early spring. The petals and sepals are white or pale pink — the pouch is a darker shade of pink. It will grow in Intermediate or Warm conditions.

P. insigne

Plain green-leaved type. A single 5 in. (12.5 cm) wide flower appears on the spike. The upper sepal of this shiny bloom is yellow with large brown spots. The narrow brown petals are striped and the amber-coloured pouch has brown veins. A vigorous plant which likes Cool conditions.

P. niveum

Mottled-leaved type. This species is more difficult to grow than the others described here. The rounded white flowers have tiny purple spots. Thrives in Warm conditions.

P. rothschildianum

Plain green-leaved type. A showpiece of the orchid world. The petals when spread out produce a flower which is 12 in. (30 cm) wide, and the colouring is dramatic. The greenish upper sepal is boldly striped in dark brown – the narrow petals are even darker. Several blooms appear on each spike. It needs rather more light than the other species.

P. Transvaal

Mottled-leaved type. A hybrid of *P. rothschildianum* — easier to grow, but less impressive. The upper sepal is yellow with red stripes, and the narrow hairy petals are yellow with red spots.

P. Pinocchio

Plain green-leaved type. A compact hybrid with colourful flowers. Several 3 in. (7.5 cm) blooms appear on the spike, blooming in succession. The upper sepal is yellowish green — the hairy-edged narrow petals are spotted. The pouch is a blend of yellow and pink.

P. Maudiae

Mottled-leaved type. A single 4 in. (10 cm) wide bloom is borne above the attractive foliage. There are many types and hybrids — the basic one has green-striped white flowers with a pale green pouch. The Coloratum group has purple-striped flowers — the Vinicolor group has red or brown flowers.

P. Saint Swithin

Plain green-leaved type. The white flowers are large with bold brown stripes — the narrow twisted petals hang downwards. Its *P. rothschildianum* ancestry is obvious, but it is easier to grow. It needs rather more light than most other hybrids.

ORCHID MISCELLANY

The Ghost Orchid

Dendrophyllax lindenii in full flower is a sight to remember, but unfortunately you are unlikely to see this rarity in its native home. Its matted roots cling to trees growing in the swamps of Florida and Cuba, and the odd feature is that there are no leaves — it is the job of the roots to take in water and minerals, manufacture carbohydrates and produce the nutrients the plant needs.

In summer the sweet-smelling flowers appear, and these blooms appear to float in the air — hence the common name. The lip bears leg-like tails and the reason for the alternative name of Frog Orchid is obvious.

Paphiopedilum Saint Swithin

Paphiopedilum Philippinense

PHALAENOPSIS

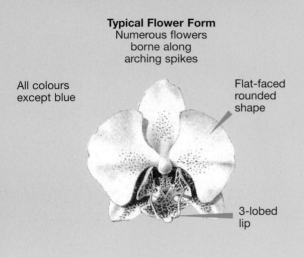

Typical Flower Form
Numerous flowers
borne along
arching spikes

All colours
except blue

Flat-faced
rounded
shape

3-lobed
lip

Pronunciation: fal-ee-**NOP**-sis

Common Name(s): Moth Orchid

Abbreviation: Phal.

Growth Type: Monopodial

Natural Habitat: On trees (rarely rocks) in tropical Asia and Australia

Ease of Cultivation: Easy

Flowering Season: No special season — can occur at any time. A collection can provide year-round flowers

Light: Reasonably bright light, but away from direct sunlight

Temperature: Warm conditions — low temperature will inhibit flowering

Watering: Year round. Compost should be kept moist, but never let it become waterlogged

Resting Period: Not needed, but a few weeks of cooler conditons at about 60°-65°F (16°-18°C) in autumn is useful

The fact that most of the orchids in homes throughout Britain and the U.S are hybrids of this genus underlines the extraordinary growth in their popularity. The Moth Orchid has transformed how we regard orchids — they are now seen as house plants for anyone and not just as expensive plants for the knowledgeable gardener.

The reason for this Moth Orchid explosion is the realisation that they thrive in the average living room — the warmth provided by central heating is ideal and so is the relatively low light intensity. In addition there is a floral display which lasts for months and the promise of repeat flowering during the year.

The floral spike which rises above the fleshy leaves is usually branched and the 2-5 in. (5-12.5 cm) wide blooms of the hybrids have large petals which overlap the sepals. The species are much less popular and here there is often a starry shape. Where space is limited you can buy one of the attractive miniature hybrids which are now available.

These orchids require moist air and so it may be necessary to increase the humidity around the leaves. Mist with care — this should be done in the morning and do make sure that no water collects at the base of the leaves.

When the last flower on the spike has faded it is time to cut back to about an inch above a node (small bump) which is below the section of the spike which has flowered. A secondary spike will usually be produced to give you a second flush of flowers.

Stake the spike with a thin cane before the flowers open and do not stand the pot outdoors. Repot only when really necessary and do not cut off the fleshy roots growing over the side of the pot. Keikis often appear — use these to produce new plants (see page 36).

PHALAENOPSIS SPECIES & HYBRIDS

P. equestris
The smallest commercially-available species which is noted for its ease of cultivation and abundant production of keikis. The branched spikes bear sprays of 1 in. (2.5 cm) wide flowers. The usual colour is white or pale pink with a lavender blush at the base of the petals and sepals.

P. violacea
The short spikes bear 2 in. (5 cm) wide starry flowers which are fragrant. The greenish-white sepals and petals are carmine red at the base — the lip is purple. It is more difficult to grow than the other species listed here.

P. schilleriana

An attractive tall species with two outstanding features. The silver-marked green foliage is decorative, and the branched spike bears scores of 3 in. (7.5 cm) wide fragrant flowers. The pale pink sepals and petals have red markings.

P. lueddemanniana

The 2 in. (5 cm) wide fragrant flowers are borne in succession on the 18 in. (45 cm) spike. There are a number of colour variations of these long-lasting blooms — the usual form has pale yellow petals and sepals with dark red spots and bars.

P. Kathleen Ai

This white or pale pink hybrid has red stripes on the sepals, petals and lip. The 3 in. (7.5 cm) wide flowers are eye-catching — Kathleen Ai has been widely used in hybridisation and is the parent of many modern candy-striped hybrid groups.

P. Petite Snow

Despite its name, this miniature bears pink and not white flowers. Many 2 in. (5 cm) wide blooms are borne on the 8 in. (20 cm) spikes. The lip is a blend of red and gold.

P. Lipperose

A pink hybrid which has given rise to numerous modern pink types. The 3 in. (7.5 cm) wide flowers have pale pink sepals and petals and darker pink veins. The ornately-shaped lip is a blend of white, pink and gold with red spots and bars.

P. Orchid World

This classic hybrid has a number of colour forms. The one you are most likely to find has a yellowish-green background on which there is a pattern of dark red spots and bars. These flowers open in succession.

ORCHID MISCELLANY

Viagra — orchid style

*For hundreds of years **Orchis mascula** and related species were used to produce love potions in Scotland, Ireland, New England etc. In the Middle East the orchid tubers were ground and the powder mixed with milk, honey and ginger to produce saloop — an aphrodisiac served in saloop saloons in Persia and Turkey. Fortunately for orchid conservation the 18th century saloop parlours of London are no more, but saloop production still continues in some parts of the world.*

Phalaenopsis lueddemanniana

Phalaenopsis Bonnie Vasquez

PHRAGMIPEDIUM

Pronunciation: frag-me-**PEE**-dee-um

Common Name(s): Slipper Orchid

Abbreviation: Phrag.

Growth Type: Sympodial

Natural Habitat: On the ground or on rocks and trees in tropical America

Ease of Cultivation: Modern hybrids are easy — some species can be difficult

Flowering Season: Depends on type — spring to autumn is the usual season

Light: Shade from direct sunlight — bright light in winter

Temperature: Warm conditions, but some will cope with Intermediate temperatures

Watering: Year round. Compost must be kept moist and not allowed to dry out. See page 20 for details

Resting Period: Not needed, but reduce feeding in winter

Typical Flower Form
Masses of fluttering flowers on top of tall, arching stems

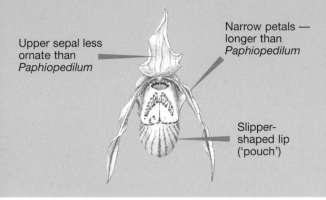

Upper sepal less ornate than *Paphiopedilum*

Narrow petals — longer than *Paphiopedilum*

Slipper-shaped lip ('pouch')

Illustrated above is one of the standard species of this American orchid. At first sight it could be mistaken for the much more popular Asian Slipper Orchid (pages 104-107) — there is a distinctive pouch and a pair of narrow petals. But there are key differences — the ribbon-like petals are unusually long and the colours are drab greys and browns. The plants are tall and belong in the greenhouse and not on a windowsill.

The long-lasting blooms open in succession — the spike may stay in flower for many months. There are no pseudobulbs and this is one of the few orchids which thrives under wet conditions, but do not mist the leaves.

Things changed in the 1980s with the discovery of the red-flowered *P. besseae*. It has produced brightly-coloured hybrids with short-petalled and large-pouched blooms.

PHRAGMIPEDIUM SPECIES & HYBRIDS

P. besseae
An unusual species in several ways. The red or bright orange colouring is unique, with petals which are short and broad. Several 2 in. (5 cm) wide blooms appear on the spike in summer or autumn.

P. Grande

A greenish-brown hybrid which first appeared over 100 years ago. The twisted ribbon-like petals hang down to 12 in. (30 cm) or more, and even longer in its natural habitat. The long upper sepal droops over the pouch.

P. Eric Young
A 5 in. (12.5 cm) wide beauty, considered by many to be the best of all the hybrids.

PLEIONE

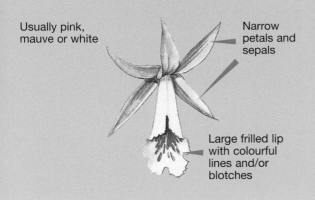

Typical Flower Form
Cattleya-like flower
on a short spike

Usually pink,
mauve or white

Narrow
petals and
sepals

Large frilled lip
with colourful
lines and/or
blotches

Pronunciation: plee-**OH**-nee

Common Name(s): Indian Crocus

Abbreviation: —

Growth Type: Sympodial

Natural Habitat: On the ground (occasionally on rocks and trees) in temperate Asia

Ease of Cultivation: Popular ones are easy — but some species can be challenging

Flowering Season: Spring, except *P. praecox* which flowers in autumn

Light: Bright light — shade from direct sunlight

Temperature: Cool conditions — unsuitable for a heated greenhouse or centrally-heated room

Watering: Outdoors — water in dry weather. In pots, water regularly during growing season — not at all in winter

Resting Period: Winter. Do not water unless pseudobulbs begin to shrivel. Keep cool but frost-free

The large flowers of this dwarf orchid are a delight in the spring, but you must choose the right home. A north-facing windowsill in an unheated room is ideal and so is a cold greenhouse or alpine house. Growing them in the garden is a risky business — you need a mild locality and free-draining soil. Protect with a cloche from autumn to spring.

Plant the dormant bulb (really a pseudobulb) in a shallow pot filled with orchid compost — bury about half of it and water carefully until the leaf has started to grow. The 4-6 in. (10-15 cm) spike bears a single 2-3 in. (5-7.5 cm) wide flower which lasts for about a week. The pot can be stood outdoors in a sheltered spot in summer.

In autumn the foliage is shed and the plant is now dormant. Repot every year before new growth begins — throw away shrivelled pseudobulbs. Plant pseudobulbs 1 in. (2.5 cm) apart.

PLEIONE SPECIES & HYBRIDS

P. speciosa

The species with the brightest petals and sepals — they are a rich pink and surround the yellow-crested lip. A small plant, growing only 4 in. (10 cm) high.

P. formosana

The popular choice with varieties in pink, mauve or white. The brown-spotted pale lip has a yellow throat. The pseudobulb is ball-shaped.

P. Shantung

This is the one to buy if you want a change from the usual white, pink or lilac. The petals and sepals are yellow or apricot, depending on the cultivar, and the yellow or white lip has bold red markings.

P. Versailles

An old hybrid with mauve-pink petals — the inside of the lip is covered with red streaks and spots.

SOPHRONITIS

Typical Flower Form
Rounded flowers
on dwarf plants

Red or
orange

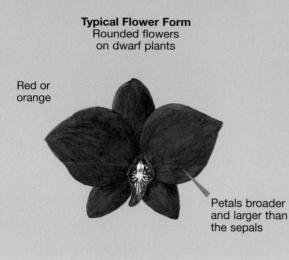

Petals broader
and larger than
the sepals

Pronunciation: sof-ron-**EYE**-tiss

Common Name(s): —

Abbreviation: S.

Growth Type: Sympodial

Natural Habitat: On trees and rocks in tropical America

Ease of Cultivation: Species can be challenging — hybrids are easier

Flowering Season: Depends on type

Light: Bright winter light, but shade from summer sun

Temperature: Intermediate conditions are ideal for nearly all types. See page 16 for details

Watering: Year round. Keep compost moist but not waterlogged during growing season. Keep drier in winter

Resting Period: Not needed, but reduce water and feeding in winter

There are two notable features — it is unusually compact and the flower colour is generally bright red. There are about seven species and a few are commercially available, but they are not often seen in collections. The 2 in. (5 cm) wide flowers are quite plain, and they are not easy to grow. They need moist air and flowering is temperamental.

This genus comes into its own as a parent of many intergeneric hybrids. There are a number of attractive *Sophrocattleya* hybrids — the popular choice is *Sophrolaeliocattleya* (Slc.). From *Cattleya* comes the dramatic shape of the flowers, *Laelia* provides the free-flowering habit and the *Sophronitis* contribution is the red or purple coloration of the blooms. These intergeneric hybrids are more vigorous and easier to grow than species such as *S. cernua* and *S. coccinea*.

SOPHRONITIS SPECIES & INTERGENERIC HYBRIDS

S. coccinea

The most popular species. The long-lasting flowers are borne singly — scarlet with yellow stripes on the lip. Varieties in other colours are available, including yellow and apricot.

Sophrocattleya Crystelle Smith

This hybrid is one of the better known examples of a *Sophronitis* x *Cattleya* cross. The petals are pink or salmon and the attractive lip is yellow with red markings.

Sophrolaeliocattleya Jewel Box

A minicatt, growing only a few inches high and bearing many relatively large flowers. Red is the usual colour but there are also orange and yellow types. The dwarf habit is derived from the *Sophronitis* parent.

Sophrolaeliocattleya Hazel Boyd

Large, perfumed flowers on a 4 in. (10 cm) plant. The petals and sepals are yellow or orange and the lip is deep red.

STANHOPEA

Typical Flower Form
Large flowers
on pendent spikes

Fragrant

Some or all
sepals and
petals are
swept back

Long ornate
lip

Pronunciation: stan-**HOPE**-ee-ah

Common Name(s): —

Abbreviation: Stan.

Growth Type: Sympodial

Natural Habitat: On trees and on the ground in tropical America

Ease of Cultivation: Most species are easy

Flowering Season: Depends on type — summer is the usual time

Light: Bright light in winter, but shade is necessary in summer

Temperature: Intermediate as a general rule — see page 16 for details

Watering: Water regularly during the growing season. Keep compost moist but not waterlogged

Resting Period: Flowering period. Reduce water when in flower, but do not allow the leaves to wilt

Few orchids are more eye-catching than a well-grown *Stanhopea* in its hanging basket in a greenhouse. The spikes grow down through the compost as well as out through the sides, and bear very fragrant and extremely bizarre blooms in summer. They may be white or highly coloured, plain or spotted with waxy flower parts which look distinctly untidy.

Eye-catching, then, but there is a serious drawback which keeps the plant out of many collections — each bloom lasts for only a few days. Despite this, many species and hybrids are available — their fragrance, size and unusual growth habit make them a worthwhile choice. Flowers open in succession so the floral display can last for several weeks.

Oddly, the plant grows actively in winter and rests in summer when in bloom. Grow on a slab (see page 31) or in a wood or wire basket, but do not house the plant in a pot.

STANHOPEA SPECIES

S. wardii
The El Toro Orchid flower is 4 in. (10 cm) wide with brown-spotted orange petals and sepals. The complex golden yellow lip has two large red spots at the base. Each spike bears 6-8 blooms.

S. oculata
The short spike bears a number of flowers which are smaller than usual. The 3 in. (7.5 cm) wide bloom is yellow with small dark spots — the cream lip is orange at the base.

S. tigrina

A pair of 7 in. (17.5 cm) wide flowers are borne on each spike of this most popular *Stanhopea* species. The pale yellow petals and sepals are splashed with deep red patches — the white lip has purple spots.

S. grandiflora
The flowers are up to 6 in. (15 cm) across. The petals and sepals are white — the lip has red streaks.

VANDA

Typical Flower Form
Clusters of flat-faced
flowers on upright spikes

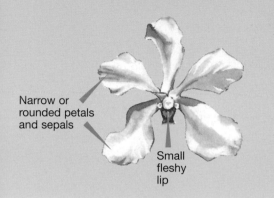

Narrow or
rounded petals
and sepals

Small
fleshy
lip

Pronunciation: VAN-dah

Common Name(s): —

Abbreviation: V.

Growth Type: Monopodial

Natural Habitat: On trees (occasionally rocks) in tropical Asia and Australia

Ease of Cultivation: Not easy — needs winter warmth, bright light and high humidity

Flowering Season: Depends on type — usually spring and summer

Light: Bright and sunny, but protect from direct summer sun

Temperature: Warm for most types — blue ones are suitable for Intermediate conditions

Watering: Year round — do not let the compost dry out. Reduce watering in winter. See page 20 for details

Resting Period: Not needed, but reduce water in winter

These orchids are to be seen in countless gardens throughout the tropics, but they are rarely seen in living rooms in temperate regions. The reasons are that the air is too dry and the light intensity is too low. You can try a hybrid near a lightly-screened south-facing window or in a heated greenhouse. You will have to mist the aerial roots regularly.

The thick upright stem bears two ranks of leaves — long aerial roots grow down from the axils. There are two types of foliage — choose a plant with strap-like leaves as the cylindrical-leaved ones need tropical conditions. Grow in a basket — in a container add fresh compost to the surface rather than repotting.

Cut off the top part of a leggy plant and pot up the cutting — leave the aerial roots intact. *Vanda* has produced a number of intergeneric hybrids — *Ascocenda* (page 66) is the most popular one. These hybrids are more compact and easier to grow than the species.

VANDA SPECIES & HYBRIDS

V. sanderiana

A colourful species for the Warm greenhouse. The rounded flowers are 3-4 in. (7.5-10 cm) wide. The upper part of the bloom is white or pale pink — the lower pale brown part is heavily veined and spotted.

V. coerulea

The Blue Orchid, although its colour is lavender rather than blue. The pale petals and sepals are netted with darker lines — the lip is purple. The 3-4 in. (7.5-10 cm) wide flowers are borne on 1½ ft (45 cm) spikes.

V. tigrina

The white or pale yellow 2 in. (5 cm) wide blooms are heavily marked with red spots and lines — the lip is purple. The winter flowers are fragrant.

V. Rothschildiana

The *Vanda* you are most likely to find for sale will be a hybrid, and this one is the favourite. It combines the netting and attractive colouring of *V. coerulea* with the attractive rounded shape of *V. sanderiana*. The flowers are 3-5 in. (7.5-12.5 cm) wide and it will thrive in Intermediate conditions. Regular feeding is required.

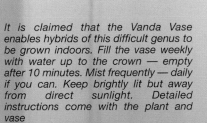

It is claimed that the Vanda Vase enables hybrids of this difficult genus to be grown indoors. Fill the vase weekly with water up to the crown — empty after 10 minutes. Mist frequently — daily if you can. Keep brightly lit but away from direct sunlight. Detailed instructions come with the plant and vase

VUYLSTEKEARA

Typical Flower Form
Large showy flowers
on single or branched spikes

Red with white is
the usual colour

Large wide lip
with yellow
lined base

Pronunciation: vul-**STEEK**-ee-ar-ah

Common Name(s): —

Abbreviation: Vuyl.

Growth Type: Sympodial

Natural Habitat: None — a trigeneric hybrid of *Odontoglossum, Miltonia* and *Cochlioda*

Ease of Cultivation: Easy

Flowering Season: Depends on type — usually winter or spring

Light: Summer shade is necessary — a north- or west-facing window is suitable

Temperature: Cool or Intermediate conditions — *V.* Cambria 'Plush' can be grown in a Warm environment, but all dislike temperatures over 80°F (27°C)

Watering: Keep compost moist but not water-logged. Keep drier in winter

Resting Period: Not needed, but reduce water and feeding in winter

You will find an example of *Vuylstekeara* in garden centres, DIY superstores and florists everywhere, but you will not find the genus on the label. It is sold under its hybrid group name — Cambria.

This hybrid genus was named after the Belgian nurseryman Charles Vuylsteke in 1911 and its most famous type was registered as *V.* Cambria 'Plush' in 1931. *Odontoglossum* is the most dominant parent — *Vuylstekeara* requires the same cultural conditions, and some *Odontoglossum* hybrids are occasionally sold as Cambria.

The flowers are about 4 in. (10 cm) wide and they last for many weeks. The one you can buy from your local shop makes an ideal beginner orchid for a windowsill — it will tolerate a wide temperature range and does not need a rest period. Repot every few years when not in flower — propagate by dividing the rhizomes (see page 35).

VUYLSTEKEARA HYBRIDS

V. Cambria 'Lensings Favorit'
This orchid originated from the much more popular 'Plush' cultivar of *V.* Cambria. The flowers have a similar shape, but the petals and sepals are white with red blotches and the lip is pink with a large red patch at the base.

V. Cambria 'Plush'

The Cambria on the garden centre bench. The petals and sepals are deep red edged with white and the ornate white lip is marked with red spots. Each spike bears 10-12 flowers and the plant may bloom more than once a year.

V. Cambria 'Yellow'
A change from the usual red colour — this cultivar has the same shape as 'Plush' but the flower parts are yellow and white.

V. Yokara 'Perfection'
An eye-catching hybrid in the red-purple range. The background colour is pale pink, but this is almost entirely covered with an intricate pattern of burgundy lines and spots.

Vuylstekeara Cambria
'Lensings Favorit'

ZYGOPETALUM

Pronunciation: zy-go-**PET**-ah-lum

Common Name(s): —

Abbreviation: Z.

Growth Type: Sympodial

Natural Habitat: On the ground and on trees in tropical America

Ease of Cultivation: Some are challenging, but popular ones are generally easy

Flowering Season: Depends on type — usual time is autumn or winter

Light: Bright, but away from direct sunlight. An east– or west-facing windowsill is suitable

Temperature: Intermediate or Cool conditions. See page 16 for details

Watering: Year round. Keep compost moist at all times during the growing season. Keep drier in winter

Resting Period: Not needed, but reduce water and feeding in winter

Typical Flower Form
Several highly-scented flowers on upright spikes

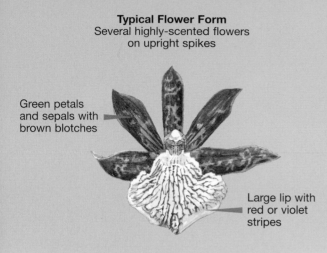

Green petals and sepals with brown blotches

Large lip with red or violet stripes

The general colour pattern illustrated above applies to nearly all the species and hybrids, but the dark brown overlay ranges from being barely present to an almost complete covering.

The spikes with their 2-3 in. (5-7.5 cm) wide flowers rise above the plum-like pseudobulbs and leaves — staking may be necessary. Most types are large and require a greenhouse or conservatory, but small ones such as *Z. crinitum* can be grown on the windowsill. The plants should not be stood outdoors in summer nor should the leaves be misted.

The plants can be cared for in the same way as *Cymbidium* and the two are sometimes grown together. Take care when repotting as the roots are fragile, and the stalks should be cut down to about 1 in. (2.5 cm) when flowering is over.

ZYGOPETALUM SPECIES & HYBRIDS

Z. intermedium
This is the species you are most likely to find in the catalogues. It is a plant for the greenhouse — the spikes are about 2½ ft (75 cm) high. The 3 in. (7.5 cm) wide flowers have narrow petals and sepals.

Z. crinitum

More compact than *Z. intermedium* and the flowers are smaller. Each spike bears about 6 blooms in spring. The petals and sepals have the typical *Zygopetalum* brown bars.

Z. Artur Elle
A compact hybrid which bears a number of spikes. As with most hybrids the colours are darker than on the species — the lip is almost covered by purple lines and blotches.

Z. Blackii
An autumn-flowering hybrid which is a truly dark orchid. The green of the sepals and petals is almost totally obscured by the near-black blotching, and the lip bears broad dark lines.

Zygopetalum Blackii

MISCELLANEOUS ORCHIDS

ANGULOA

The Tulip Orchid. The reason for the common name is immediately obvious — a single cup-shaped bloom is borne on an upright stalk above the tulip-like leaves. *A. clowesii* is the usual one — 3 in. (7.5 cm) wide fragrant yellow flowers appear in early summer. Provide Cool conditions in the greenhouse. It is a deciduous plant — allow to rest after leaf fall by not watering until growth starts in the spring.

ASPASIA

A plant for the windowsill if you can keep the air moist by misting and using a humidity tray. *A. lunata* is the most popular one — the short spike bears 2 in. (5 cm) wide starry flowers in summer. The sepals and petals are green with brown markings — the flared lip is white with purple markings. Provide Cool or Intermediate conditions and diffuse lighting. Water liberally in the growing season, but reduce watering in winter.

BIFRENARIA

A plant for a Cool or Intermediate greenhouse — some sun is needed, but not direct summer sun. *B. harrisoniae* is the only species you are likely to find — the 3 in. (7.5 cm) wide waxy flowers are creamy-white with a purple hairy lip. Spring is the usual flowering season — the blooms are long-lasting but this orchid is notoriously flower-shy. Water is required throughout the year, but reduce watering slightly in winter.

CALANTHE

There are two groups of this terrestrial orchid. The evergreen types are suitable for a Cool house — no resting period is required. *C. discolor* is an example — usual colour is brown with a white lip. The deciduous ones need Warm conditions and a sunny situation. *C. vestita* is the usual species — wide-lipped with petals and sepals in various colours. Water deciduous ones very sparingly between autumn and spring.

CATASETUM

Something different — the male and female flowers are on separate spikes or even different plants. The 2 in. (5 cm) wide flowers are creamy with brown splashes — the male ones are brighter. The arching spike bears about a dozen of these flowers in late summer. Provide Intermediate conditions — after leaf fall provide only enough water to prevent the pseudobulbs from shrivelling until spring. Bright indirect sunlight is needed.

COCHLIODA

A close relative of *Odontoglossum*. Numerous small pink or red flowers are borne on long arching spikes — Cool conditions are needed and direct sunlight should be avoided. *Cochlioda* is used in hybridisation to add red to showier orchids which lack this colour. A few species are available — *C. sanguinea* has scores of pink flowers along the spike. The orange blooms of *C. noezliana* are larger but fewer in number.

DENDROCHILUM

D. filiforme is the Chain Orchid — in spring or summer masses of tiny ivory flowers are borne in two rows along the pendent 1 ft (30 cm) long spike. Grow in a shallow pot and keep moist — provide less water in winter. It is an easy plant to grow in Cool or Intermediate conditions — some morning or evening direct sun is beneficial. *D. glumaceum* has the largest flowers. Do not repot unless it is essential.

DORITIS

D. pulcherrima is a relative of the much more popular Moth Orchid (page 108). Tall spikes appear, each one bearing numerous magenta flowers which open in succession over a period of several months. Warm conditions and reasonably bright light are required — a plant for a centrally-heated room. The intergeneric hybrid *Doritaenopsis* (see picture above) is popular. Cut back the stalks after flowering for a second flush — see *Phalaenopsis*.

GONGORA

G. galatea has yellowish brown 2 in. (5 cm) wide flowers on long pendent spikes. These fragrant blooms last for about a week and usually appear in late summer. The shape of some species (e.g *G. maculata*) is unusual, resembling a flying bird. Intermediate or Warm conditions are required and a winter rest is needed — only give enough water at this time to prevent the pseudobulbs from shrivelling. Grow in a basket.

LEMBOGLOSSUM

This starry-flowered genus is closely related to *Odontoglossum*. The tall erect spikes of *L. bictoniense* carry 2 in. (5 cm) wide fragrant blooms in summer — the brown-marked petals and sepals are narrow and the heart-shaped lip is white suffused with pink. Some shade is necessary in summer and watering should be reduced only a little in winter. Keep in a Cool greenhouse and grow in a pot or on a slab (see page 31).

LEPTOTES

An early-flowering miniature for the windowsill — it grows only an inch or two high but the flowers are 2 in. (5 cm) wide. *L. bicolor* is the usual one — the narrow sepals and petals are white and the lip is flushed with purple. *L. unicolor* has pale purple flowers. It requires Intermediate conditions and filtered sunlight. Allow the surface to dry between waterings — reduce after flowering. Grow on a slab or in a shallow pot.

MAXILLARIA

This tropical American orchid needs Intermediate conditions, protection from direct sunlight and a reduction in water after flowering. A single flower is borne on the spike, and the plants come in a range of shapes and sizes from miniatures to giants. *M. coccinea* is a red-flowering dwarf — the popular *M. tenuifolia* has red and yellow flowers. The jaw-like lip is often pale with purple or red stripes and spots.

NEOFINETIA

N. falcata is a Japanese miniature with an interesting story — its cultivation was once restricted to the Emperor and his family. The short spike bears several 1 in. (2.5 cm) wide waxy white flowers — the petals and sepals are narrow, and there is a spur behind the lip. Provide Intermediate conditions and keep the compost moist — reduce watering after flowering. The light should be bright, but screen against direct sun. A good windowsill plant.

PHAIUS

Most species are terrestrial. The only one you are likely to find is *P. tancarvillae* — the Nun's Orchid. It is a tall plant with 3 ft (90 cm) long leaves. The flower spike bears 3 in. (7.5 cm) wide flowers. The narrow sepals and petals are brown with a white reverse — the tubular red lip has a white base. Provide Intermediate conditions, filtered sun and humid air. Water freely, but more sparingly for a few weeks after flowering.

PLEUROTHALLIS

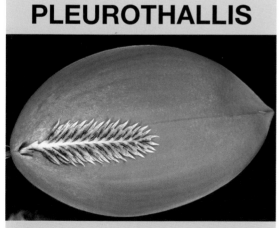

An extremely varied genus which ranges from tall-growing types to tiny ones — neither typical flower form nor standard list of requirements exists. The ones you are most likely to see are the miniatures with flowers measuring ¼ in. (5 mm) or less. With the 'frog' group the blooms sit at the base of the leaf — others bear numerous flowers on branched spikes. Generally easy to grow in a Cool house — water liberally during the growing season.

RENANTHERA

Red, orange and yellow are the dominant colours. Most are tall and leafy plants, but *R. monachica* is a dwarf with red-spotted yellow flowers. *R. bella* is rather similar, but the blooms are red — intergeneric hybrids are more popular than the species. Not easy plants to grow nor are they easy to find — provide Intermediate conditions and some morning or evening sun. Water sparingly during the resting period.

RHYNCHOSTYLIS

Foxtail Orchid is an appropriate common name — the curved 1½ ft (45 cm) long spike of *R. gigantea* bears scores of closely-packed 1 in. (2.5 cm) wide flowers in summer. Each one has purple-spotted white sepals and petals, a dark-centred lip and a spur. *R. retusa* is rather smaller. There are no pseudobulbs. Provide Warm condi-tions with indirect sunlight and keep moist during the growing season. Grow in a basket rather than a pot.

SOBRALIA

A tall-growing terrestrial orchid from S. America. The most popular species is *S. macrantha* — each spike bears about 6 flowers which measure up to 6 in. (15 cm) across. The petals and sepals are purple — the large purple lip has a white throat. The blooms open in succession — each one lasts for only a few days. Intermediate conditions, some bright sun and moist compost are required. Reduce watering for several weeks in winter.

TRICHOPILIA

The fragrant blooms hang over the side of the basket on slender spikes — the large circular lip is surrounded by the narrow petals and sepals. This compact plant rarely exceeds 6 in. (15 cm) — it needs Intermediate conditions, filtered sunlight and compost which is moist at all times. Look for *T. tortilis*, the Corkscrew Orchid. The pale purple petals and sepals are spirally twisted — the yellow-centred lip is white with brown spots.

Only a tiny fraction of the genera in the orchid world are grown commercially, and of these a mere handful are available on the High St. These mass-produced ones are, of course, included in this book together with many others which are offered for sale in Europe and the U.S. The genera described in this A-Z guide are the more popular ones, but there are scores of others. Consult the orchid grower websites for descriptions and prices for the non-listed genera below — you may have to search widely for some of them.

Ada	*Liparis*
Broughtonia	*Lockhartia*
Cirrhopetalum	*Mexicoa*
Cryptolaemus	*Promenea*
Crytorchis	*Pterostylis*
Disa	*Schomburgkia*
Euanthe	*Spathoglottis*
Eulophia	*Stenoglottis*
Habenaria	*Thunia*
Jumellea	*Zygoneria*

CHAPTER 12

INDEX

Acknowledgements

The author wishes to acknowledge the painstaking work of Gill Jackson.
Grateful acknowledgement is also made for the help received
from Barry Highland and Ian Harris (Spot On Digital Imaging Ltd) and
Lisa Smith, Tyrone McGlinchey and Linda McGlinchey (Garden World Images).
The author is also grateful for the photographs or artworks received from David Baylis,
Dr Tim Baylis, Judith Blacklock, Down House/The Bridgeman Art Library,
David Guthrie (Bluebridge Farm Studio), Hollyhouse Media, Photos Horticultural,
RHS Lindley Library, Richard Warren (Equatorial Plant Company) and Christine Wilson.